CLASSIC WALKS
— IN —
WESTERN
EUROPE

GILLIAN & JOHN SOUTER

David & Charles

A DAVID & CHARLES BOOK

First published in Great Britain in 2000 by David & Charles
Created and designed by Off the Shelf Publishing, Australia
© Off the Shelf Publishing 2000

Gillian and John Souter have asserted their right to be identified as
authors of this work in accordance with the Copyright, Designs and
Patents Act 1988.

A catalogue record for this book is available from the British Library.

ISBN 0 7153 1111 5

All photographs by Gillian Souter except:

p 21 - D. Viet - CRT Midi-Pyrénées,
courtesy of Office de Tourisme de Rocamadour;
p 57 - courtesy of Gosau Tourismusverband;
p 100 - courtesy of Todtnau Kurhaus;
pp 125, 129 & 131 - John Morrison, True North;
p138 (lower) - Charles & Betty Marsh.

Filmwork by Acumen Overseas, Singapore
Printed in Singapore by Kyodo Printing
for David & Charles
Brunel House   Newton Abbot   Devon

Photographs without captions:
   Page 2: near St Chély d'Aubrac;
   Opposite: *(top)* Assisi, Umbria;
   (middle) Lobhörnhutte, Bernese Alps;
   (bottom) near Ubraye, Provence;
   Page 7: a path in the Italian Dolomites.

CONTENTS

An Introduction

Over the past centuries, our perspective on travel has shifted markedly. Perhaps the first people to travel in large numbers for reasons other than trade or subsistence were the pilgrims of the middle ages. These were, in some sense, the first tourists and making a pilgrimage became an extremely popular pastime. Although there was always a destination where redemption could be earned, an essential part of the spiritual healing process was the journey itself. No doubt it also broadened many a narrow mind, as people from different social groups came into contact and passed through foreign landscapes.

When pilgrimage declined due to wars and changing religious tenets, travel for pleasure became the preserve of the wealthy and it wasn't until the introduction of fast modes of transport—the carriage, the car, the train and of course the plane—that mass tourism became a phenomenon. We can, if we choose, visit a dozen cities in as many days and strangely, some do. It's understandable: our lives are hectic and leisure time is limited. However, these are equally good reasons to travel in a different manner, avoiding airports and motorways as much as possible and resorting instead to the footpath and the country lane, becoming modern-day pilgrims.

If you've never spent four or five days in a foreign land with a subset of your belongings on your back and armed merely with a map, you have much to discover. Your concerns are quickly reduced to whether it will rain, where you'll stop for lunch, which way is the path. Problems that seemed insurmountable only a short time before either diminish in importance or resolve themselves altogether as you tramp on. The exertion of a day's walk gives you a wondrous appetite for the local cuisine and earns you a solid sleep that refreshes you for the next day. You will find that walking daily becomes addictive and what you thought might be a bit over-long or strenuous is pleasantly achieved.

All this ignores what you are walking through, of course. Nature, thanks in part to the Romantic poets of the 19th century, is now perceived as a positive force rather than something inherently hostile which must be tamed. There are few remnants of absolute wilderness in western Europe and the traveller who hopes for idyllic arcadia will be walking for a long time in search of it. However, there are parts where human intervention has been minimal, especially in more mountainous regions, or where cultivation has

The European countryside can be traversed on paths once used for herding stock and trading.

WALKS IN WESTERN EUROPE

1 The Dordogne
2 Way of St Jacques
3 The Verdon Gorge
4 The Salzkammergut
5 Umbrian Hilltowns

6 The Dolomites
7 The Cinque Terre
8 The High Black Forest
9 Saxon Switzerland

10 Heart of Scotland
11 The Lake District
12 The Bernese Alps
13 The High Alpujarras

resulted in landscapes of great beauty. There are also places where human culture has created sites which now imbue the landscape with history: when these are stumbled upon in a remote setting, the impact is far, far greater than when you troop off a coach and queue to visit such places.

Walking is not a means of avoiding people: people *en masse* yes, but not people altogether. When you haven't seen a soul save your companion for several hours, other people suddenly become much more interesting beings. We have treasured memories of people we have met while temporarily lost in regions all over Europe. A few phrases of local language make such encounters more enjoyable (and fruitful), but you will find you do not need to master the subtleties of a language to enjoy a *pastis* or a *birra* in the bar each evening. Europe, despite its increasing economic unity, remains culturally diverse, especially so away from its cities. Walking through a country allows you to come a little nearer to understanding its features, both geographical and cultural, while you soothe your soul.

WALKING PATHS IN WESTERN EUROPE

Over the centuries of settlement, paths crisscrossing regions of Europe have been developed for droving livestock and for movement and trade between villages. In some countries, these paths remain unmarked but well-trod: the mule tracks in the Alpujarras are a good example. In countries where hiking has become a popular pastime, such as France, Germany and Britain, many of these paths have been maintained as waymarked footpaths. In some cases, local footpaths have been incorporated into long-distance paths from which, in turn, the European Ramblers Association has created half a dozen long-distance paths that traverse much of the continent. One such, the E4, is encountered briefly on our route in the Salzkammergut and again on the Way of St Jacques, several countries away.

Perhaps the best model for path marking is France; indeed many countries have adapted its system of waymarking. In France, national long-distance paths (*grandes randonnées* or GR) are allocated a number and waymarked with horizontal red-and-white stripes. Local paths (*petites randonnées* or PR) are marked with yellow stripes. A combination–red and yellow stripes–indicates that it is a regional long-distance path. Variations on this theme are used to indicate direction: see the diagram opposite. These marks are daubed on trees, rocks or walls and you need to develop an eye for them. Where the walks in this book follow a waymarked path, we have given less detailed directions.

We have deliberately chosen walks in regions with different climates and geography. Several are in a Mediterranean setting–Provence, Liguria, Umbria–where rainfall is low and temperatures range from mild to hot. A walk in the Spanish Alpujarras combines elements of a Mediterranean climate with aspects of high altitude. The regions walked in Britain are Atlantic-affected: the weather here is changeable, with heavy rainfall. Mid-Continent–in the Dordogne, the Aubrac and in Germany–you can expect a lower rainfall with a greater range of temperatures. Finally, there are

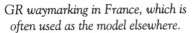

GR waymarking in France, which is often used as the model elsewhere.

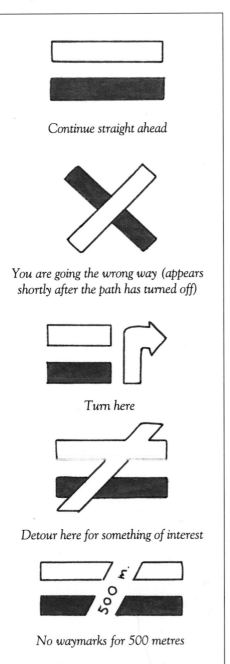

Continue straight ahead

You are going the wrong way (appears shortly after the path has turned off)

Turn here

Detour here for something of interest

No waymarks for 500 metres

*Many countries maintain
long-distance walking paths and
actively encourage hikers.*

A LUGGAGE CHECKLIST

- a comfortable pack
- sturdy boots
- thick socks
- a waterproof jacket
- a water bottle
- sunscreen
- sunglasses
- a compass
- a whistle
- a penknife
- a first aid kit

walks in Alpine regions–the Dolomites, the Salzkammergut, the Bernese Oberland–where snow rules out walking in winter and where the terrain is necessarily steeper. All the walks included here are below the 2700-metre level (and most are below 2000 m) and no specialist equipment or climbing skills are required.

Most of the walks we have described are one-way, but all of these allow for return to a starting point by public transport, in case you need to re-cover luggage or a car. For those readers with limited time or ambition, the chapter endnotes includes a short variant of the walk. In areas of higher altitude, where the weather is less predictable, we have chosen a single town as a base from which to venture on day walks. These sometimes involve a short trip by public transport to a starting point, but most begin from the outskirts of that town.

BEFORE YOUR JOURNEY

This book has been written for people who enjoy a full day's walk and don't want to deprive themselves of a well-cooked meal and a comfortable bed. If you are happy with less luxury then you might consider taking camping equipment. This gives you additional freedom but adds weight to your pack. If your walk is part of a longer trip, consider leaving the bulk of your lug-gage at the left-luggage counter of a railway station or with a reliable hotel, and then carry your walking requirements in a largish day-pack. This may require you to wash clothing along the way, but it makes the walking far more enjoyable. This is how we usually undertake our journeys and we can thoroughly recommend it. The chapter endnotes suggest a place for leav-ing surplus luggage.

If you feel uncertain about walking in an unfamiliar region, you might consider booking a guided group walk with a specialist travel company, of which there are several. A good compromise, however, is to book a 'self guided' or 'luggage-free' package, in which the company (or a local tourist office) organises your accommodation, provides you with detailed maps and notes, and arranges for your luggage to be moved to the next night's destination. Many of the areas in this book can be walked in this way.

A grid summarising the walks in this book can be found on page 160. Once you've chosen the area where you wish to walk, gather as much information as you can before you get there. Many useful sites are appear-ing on the internet with information on local accommodation and trans-port; the chapter endnotes list some of these. If possible, buy the relevant maps in advance along with any detailed guide books you might want for extra reading. We have listed contact details for local tourist authorities at the end of each chapter, so contact them if you need information on how to get to your starting point or if you want to book accommodation in advance. Photocopy the relevant pages of this book and take them with you in a plastic sleeve. When read in conjunction with a detailed map and the path's waymarkings, the route description should see you safely to each day's destination.

The network of public transport throughout western Europe is excellent and we have given basic details on how to reach the paths described. Once you've reached a region, collect any timetables that might prove useful at the completion of the walk, or as emergency transport on wet days. A couple of the walks in more urbanised areas have short sections which you might want to skip, either by bus or by taxi.

Essential items are a comfortable pack, a pair of sturdy, broken-in boots, thick socks, a waterproof jacket, a water bottle, sunscreen and sunglasses (ultraviolet increases at high altitudes), a compass (and a basic knowledge of how to use it), a whistle, and a penknife with a corkscrew. Depending on the season, you might need gloves, a warm hat, a thick sweater or conversely, a sunhat, shorts and swimwear. A map holder is useful for keeping maps dry and handy. When in a foreign-speaking country, a phrase book is a necessary evil. If your boots are a recent acquisition, pack blister plasters.

Most important of all, to enjoy distance walking over a number of days, you must have a certain level of fitness and stamina. We have given rough estimates each day for the number of hours spent walking as well as the distance covered, as in mountainous terrain this is the more important figure. In preparation, make sure you have walked steadily for such a length of time on several recent weekend outings.

ON THE WALK

Simple accommodation is available in each of the suggested overnight stops, although this is sometimes limited: check the notes for details. If you are travelling in peak holiday season—usually July and August—you might be wise to book hotels before you leave, or when you reach a nearby tourist centre. The ideal season to walk is generally in the months preceding and after this peak time, but how far you can stray either side of summer will be dictated by the climate of the region. The chapter endnotes provide population estimates for each village *en route*; those in bold are the overnight stops. Their relative size should be some indication of the amenities they offer, including banks, post offices and so on.

One of the great pleasures of travel is tasting regional cuisines and after a day's walk you should indulge yourself with a good evening meal. Don't assume, however, that you can buy a cooked meal in the middle of the day. Instead, buy supplies each morning and enjoy a picnic of fresh bread with local cheeses, meats, fruit and regional delicacies. Always carry a good supply of water, filling up at supplies clearly marked as potable. If you're uncertain, bottled water is an inexpensive safeguard. Carry a plastic bag so you can dispose of your rubbish when you reach the next village.

The importance of protecting the environment through which you travel goes without saying. Please respect the local people's rights by obeying signs, closing gates and not damaging crops, livestock, or sources of wild food. Guard against fires, especially in forested areas, and take care not to harm the wildlife, terrain and natural vegetation which collectively make up the walker's balm.

The ideal load contains only enough to make life comfortable and walking a pleasure.

THE DORDOGNE

A magnificent walk along the quiet paths of the Dordogne river valley, replete with grand castles, fortified bastide towns and other vestiges of the Hundred Years War, ending at the spectacular site of Rocamadour.

The Dordogne is one of France's longest rivers and is said by many to be its most beautiful. This five-day walk is centred on the upper Dordogne river valley and surrounding plateaux formerly known as Haut-Quercy. Unmarred by large industrial cities and away from teaming tourist haunts, the area provides a wealth of opportunity for the walker and is crisscrossed by long distance footpaths, several of which form the basis of this near-circular walk. The walker will discover uncluttered landscapes of wooded hills and lush farmland, open limestone plateaux or *causses* carved through by pretty river valleys and deeper gorges, and unspoilt medieval villages linked by twisting and untrafficked lanes. The valleys of the Dordogne, the Cère, the Bave, the Autoire and the Alzou all make for superb walking. The Martel and Gramat Causses, though more remote and arid, are equally interesting; the Gouffre de Padirac, a dramatic chasm on the Gramat Causse, is one of France's natural wonders.

The region's tranquillity is largely the result of depopulation. The rural exodus has continued throughout the twentieth century, stemmed only partly by the advent of tourism. The quietude is in stark contrast to the region's tumultuous past, evidence of which can be seen in the fortifications surrounding its châteaux, churches and indeed its towns and villages. This was long disputed territory with ownership alternating between the English Plantagenets and French Capetians, the river Dordogne acting as a natural dividing line. Quercy was ceded to the English by the 1259 Treaty of Paris but fighting during the Hundred Years War restored it to French ownership in 1369. Centuries on, the area was racked by the intermittent Wars of Religion between Huguenot Protestants and Catholics.

This route encompasses many sites attesting to these bloody struggles: old, walled towns such as Martel, Turenne and Rocamadour; the *bastide* (planned) town of Bretenoux; Castelnau-Bretenoux Château and the ruins of other fortifications. The walker will also encounter exquisite artifacts which once drew fervent pilgrims through these parts on their way both to Santiago de Compostela and to the Shrine of St Amadour at Rocamadour

The countryside through which the Dordogne flows: equally rich in history and pastoral beauty.

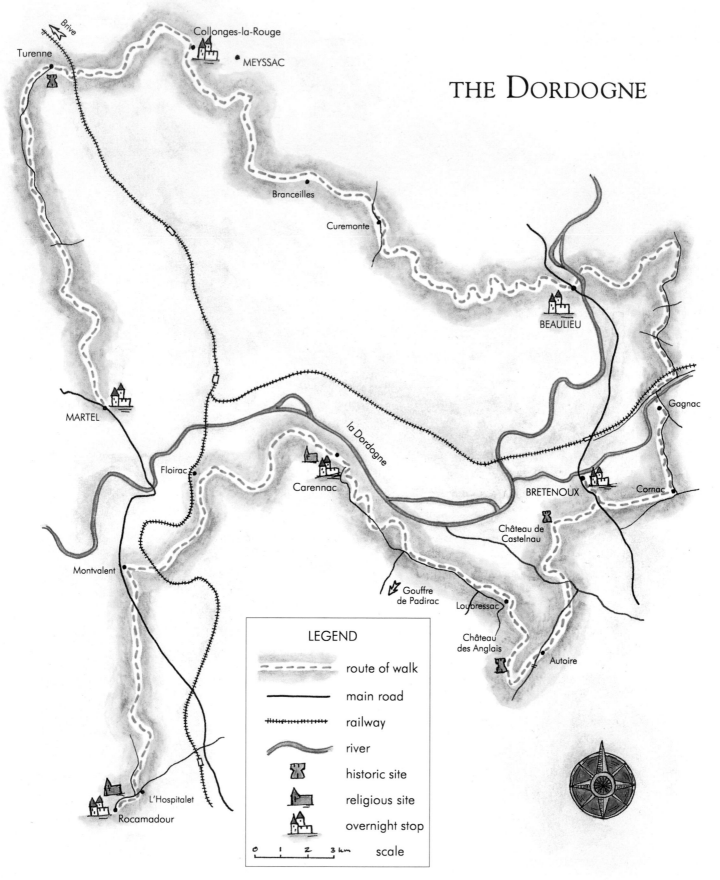

THE DORDOGNE

Brive

Turenne

Collonges-la-Rouge

MEYSSAC

Branceilles

Curemonte

BEAULIEU

Gagnac

MARTEL

la Dordogne

Floirac

Carennac

BRETENOUX

Cornac

Château de
Castelnau

Montvalent

Gouffre
de Padirac

Loubressac

Château
des Anglais

Autoire

L'Hospitalet

Rocamadour

LEGEND

route of walk

main road

railway

river

historic site

religious site

overnight stop

0   1   2   3 km   scale

where this walk concludes. The Quercy Romanesque style of religious architecture was rich in sculptural decoration, creating carved doorways known as *tympana* which were then among the most beautiful in France. Excellent examples are to be seen at Martel, Collonges-la-Rouge, Beaulieu-sur-Dordogne and Carennac.

Much of the time you will be walking through pastureland, farmland and orchards, for the Dordogne is predominantly an agricultural area. Walnuts, tobacco, strawberries, ducks and geese (for *foie gras*) and maize (to fatten the ducks and geese) are all plentiful and a hardy breed of sheep is grazed on the causse pastureland. Dining certainly is no hardship in the Dordogne, famed for one of France's greatest regional cuisines.

DAY ONE - MARTEL TO COLLONGES-LA-ROUGE (21.5 KM; 5.5 HRS)

The first day's journey is northwards over the Martel Causse, always following the GR (*grande randonnée*) 446-480 through undulating farmland and woodland to the ancient hilltown of Turenne and then east to nearby Collonges-la-Rouge with its unique red sandstone architecture.

Our route begins in Martel, a picturesque market town 7 km by road from the St Denis-pres-Martel railway station. Martel is known as the 'town of seven towers' and many of its well-preserved medieval buildings were once protected by its double perimeter walls. You should take time to inspect the Gothic St-Maur church with its excellent Romanesque tympanum depicting the Last Judgement, its buttressed belltower and other towers with battlements. There is an 18th century covered market or *halle* in the Place des Consuls and the nearby town hall, the Hotel de la Raymondie, is an elegant mansion originally built as a fortress in the 13th and 14th centuries. Lunch provisions should be purchased before leaving Martel.

Leave Martel on the GR 446-480 which heads off north and can be joined from the north side of the N140 road to the right of its intersection with the D23. The path soon crosses but stays close to the D23 for about 1 km; there are good views back to Martel's distinctive skyline. The path then veers off to the left (NW) and heads into woodland and after another 1 km it swings right (NE) and later joins a minor road. Turn left at a T-junction, crossing the stream, and follow the D23. After 500 m you turn left on a forest path which joins another minor road at the hamlet of Maslafon. From here it is under 5 km to the hamlet of Hôpital-St-Jean, the site of a medieval leper hospice, first on woodland paths and then following the D23 once more.

About 2 km north of Hôpital-St-Jean, you leave the region of Midi-Pyrénées and enter Limousin. At the hamlet of la Gironie, the path forks left following the D150 towards Turenne before crossing the D8 to climb the narrow cobbled streets of the medieval village. Overlooking a delightful landscape of wood and meadowland, the hilltop town of Turenne nestles sleepily around the ruins of its fortified castle. Its size belies its former importance as the capital of the viscounty of Turenne which held power over more than 1200 villages and abbeys in the 15th century. Under the La Tour d'Auvergne dynasty, Turenne remained the last independent feudal fiefdom in France

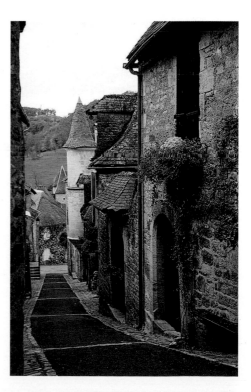

A substantial doorway in Martel (above) and one of Turenne's quaint narrow lanes (below).

until the ninth viscount sold the viscounty to Louis XV in 1738. All that remains of the fortress are the 11th century Tour de Cesar (with panoramic views east to the Monts du Cantal) and the 13th century Tour de l'Horloge. The 15th and 16th century town houses surrounding the Place de la Halle attest to Turenne's former wealth.

Our route leaves the town eastwards downhill along a road which passes under a railway line after about 1 km. Soon after turn right onto a minor road and in 500 m turn right again onto a path through a strip of woodland and orchards to rejoin a road and pass through the small hamlet of Ligneyrac. Continue past the church and, as the road bends sharply, the path continues off to the left. About 1 km further on, the path veers left and skirts a hill, above a road, to reach orchards. From here the route follows minor roads into Collonges-la-Rouge. The distant prospect of Collonges in the late afternoon light is extraordinarily beautiful, its deep red sandstone buildings set amidst verdant countryside. The development of the village dates back to the 8th century but

The Rennaissance buildings of Collonges-la-Rouges.

later the village became a halt for pilgrims en route to Santiago de Compostela in Spain. Collonges is graced by châteaux and manor houses with pepper-pot turrets and towers dating from the 16th century when it became the holiday retreat for Turenne's nobility. The whole village repays thorough exploration but particularly the covered market with its communal oven and the 13th century penitents' chapel. The church dates from the 11th century but was fortified during the 16th century Wars of Religion. The beautiful 12th century tympanum, in Quercy Romanesque style, is carved from white Turenne limestone, contrasting with the building's red sandstone. Nearby Meyssac, another picturesque town of red sandstone, is an alternative overnight stop.

Day Two - Collonges-la-rouge to Beaulieu (26 km; 6.5 hrs)

Still following the GR 446-480, we now journey southeast through undulating countryside and the tiny isolated villages of Branceilles and Curemonte before descending east to Beaulieu on the banks of the Dordogne.

Buy lunch provisions before leaving Collonges on the road to Saillac. In 500 m the path forks left from the road and heads SSE. For the next 10 km the route heads generally S to SE, following paths and short stretches of road through orchards, farms and woodland. The tiny settlements of Pevridieu, Cruze and Coquart are passed and Branceilles can be visited by making a short detour on the D10. Otherwise the path skirts north of the village, heading SW from the junction through orchards, crossing the Ruisseau le Maumont and veering left to follow a lane. A minor road is reached and followed right into the village of Curemonte, classified as one of 'les plus beaux villages de France'. Curemonte is set imposingly atop an escarpment overlooking the valley of the Soudoire. The village was named after one of the knights of the First Crusade in 1096, Raymond de Curemonte, and has seen little change in recent centuries. Full of turreted and towered old houses, Curemonte also boasts three churches and three châteaux.

The GR 446-480 wends through Curemonte and leaves on the D15. Soon you follow a minor road left to a T-junction. Here the path leaves the road and contours around a small hill. On reaching a crossroads, the route heads south, then 100 m on, turns left onto a footpath to the settlement of Sennac. From here, follow the road east for 1 km then turn right onto the D153 and left at the next T-junction. The route now zigzags down through woods and then on the winding D153E to pass a communications pylon. Turn left onto a minor road for a short distance then right onto an ancient cobbled mule track that descends the river valley steeply. Soon the Dordogne is glimpsed through the trees and the path descends to cross the main road (D940) and enter Beaulieu-sur-Dordogne.

Beaulieu is an attractive old riverside village which lines a gentle curve in the upper Dordogne. The village centres around its famous church, the majestic 12th century Romanesque abbey church of Sainte-Pierre, once a pilgrim halt en route to Santiago de Compostela. The south portal features a tympanum, carved from limestone around 1140, depicting Christ's second coming. Christ is represented as a triumphant Roman emperor while

A pretty château found just outside of Beaulieu.

the double lintel below depicts the seven-headed monster from the book of Revelation. Nearby, on the riverbank is the restored 12th century Chapelle des Penitents, now a religious art and history museum. Beaulieu has an open-air market on Wednesdays and Saturdays and a tourist office.

DAY THREE - BEAULIEU TO BRETENOUX (20 KM; 5 HRS)

Today's journey involves a climb out of the Dordogne valley, leaving the GR footpath to cross fertile farmland and forest on backroads before descending the valley of the Cère, joining a new GR footpath and arriving at the former bastide town of Bretenoux.

Following the GR 446-480, cross the Dordogne on a footbridge near the Chapelle des Penitents. The path crosses parkland to reach a riverside road which is followed right with beautiful views left through a vineyard to a château. After 700 m the path veers away from the river and crosses first the D116 and soon after the D41, zigzagging uphill to a communications pylon. Less than 1 km on, the route heads E along a minor road through the settlement of la Borderie. After 1 km, leave the waymarked GR route and turn right (S) at a crossroads onto a minor road. Continue on this road through two sets of crossroads to reach the bucolic hamlet of Fontmerle after about 4 km. Now descend the winding D116E, turning left (SE) at an intersection and descending more gradually towards the river Cère. Near the river, turn right onto the busier D14 and follow this through Port de Gagnac then turn left over the river and into Gagnac-sur-Cère. There are pleasant picnic spots by the river if you arrive here at lunch time. Leave Gagnac, keeping the church on your right, and soon turn left onto the D134 and left again at a small cemetery to go through Glanes, the centre of a small wine-making area. Keeping the church on your right, soon cross the D3 and continue south on a minor road to reach picturesque Cornac. Here you pick up the GR 480-652 which leaves Cornac westwards on the D134. Where the road forks, the path bisects the two roads and leads beside orchards for 2 km to reach the major D940 road. Here you detour right along the D940 for 1.3 km to reach the overnight stop of Bretenoux.

Sitting prettily astride the river Cère, Bretenoux is a *bastide* town with a well-preserved medieval centre. Bastides were the 'new towns' of the 13th century, built hurriedly in the southwest of France by both the French and English in the lead up to the Hundred Years War. Some bastides were built on near-impregnable clifftop sites while others like Bretenoux depended solely on perimeter walls punctuated with gateways and towers for their protection. All bastides were built to a grid plan around a central square which contained a wooden covered market (*halle*) and was surrounded with covered arcades (*couverts*). Old Bretenoux retains its grid plan, halle, couverts and parts of the ramparts. It has since acquired hotels, restaurants, shops and a tourist office.

DAY FOUR - BRETENOUX TO CARENNAC (25 KM; 7 HRS)

Today's is a long but spectacular walk taking in the awesome Château de Castelnau, the charming villages of Autoire, Loubressac and Carennac and

A henhouse and pigeon loft in one, high on the Gramat Causse.

The mighty bulk of the Château de Castelnau-Bretenoux.

the scenery of the Bave valley, Autoire gorge and the Gramat Causse high above. A side trip to the extraordinary Gouffre de Padirac would add an extra day to the itinerary. Buy lunch provisions before leaving.

Leave Bretenoux and return to where you left the waymarked path the previous day. Turn right onto the footpath, gently ascending through wood and farmland to reach the Château de Castelnau-Bretenoux with the village of Prudhommat lying at its foot. Visible from afar, the massive red stone bulk of Castelnau is truly imposing at close quarters. It was built in the 11th century on a spur of rock by the powerful barons of Castelnau and the huge outer fortifications (more than 5 km around the perimeter) were added during the Hundred Years War. Its sheer scale–its garrison comprised 1500 men and 100 horses–makes it one of the finest examples of medieval military architecture. Guided tours are in French; the castle is closed on Tuesdays. At its foot stands the beautiful St Louis Collegiate Church and canons' residences.

The path now descends through fertile farmland to the Bave valley, crossing the pretty river Bave after a few kilometres. You soon enter the narrow valley of the Autoire near its confluence with the Bave. Cross the river Autoire and then follow it upstream. Here, set exquisitely at the mouth of the gorge, is the delightful Quercynois village of Autoire. This is a miniature showcase of Quercy architecture, replete with turreted and towered châteaux and mansions, quaint houses, and farm buildings with elegant dovecotes (built to keep the prized pigeon droppings rather than the pigeons). The steep roofed,

Remnants of the Château des Anglais, a fortification overlooking the Autoire valley.

half-timbered buildings are constructed of Gramat limestone and have small balconies reached by stone steps. *The route leaves Autoire on a footpath behind the 10th century church of St Pierre.* Soon there is a short diversion to a superb 30 m waterfall, one of several over which the Autoire plunges from the Gramat Causse. *Returning from the waterfall, you now climb steeply out of the gorge.* At a path junction, a short diversion right takes you to the dramatic ruins of the Château des Anglais, built out of the sheer cliff face by the English during the Hundred Years War to keep watch over the gorge. The views down to Autoire are indeed spectacular. *Back at the junction, continue the ascent to the limestone plateau with wonderful views back to the natural amphitheatre of the Cirque d'Autoire. Out of the gorge, the path loops around north through the dry pastureland, eventually picking up a minor road NW towards Loubressac.*

The path skirts just to the right of Loubressac but a brief detour is warranted. Loubressac, built on a spur of rock occupied since ancient times, commands splendid views eastward to the Bave valley and north to the Château de Castelnau. It has a hotel and restaurants and would make a suitable overnight stop if you plan to visit the Gouffre de Padirac. This huge collapsed cave provides access to a subterranean river 100 m below ground and to a series of astonishing galleries which it has hollowed out of the Gramat limestone. Explored by Edouard Martel from 1889 and first opened to the public in 1898, Padirac is a deservedly popular tourist attraction (open April to early October; with guided tours). *From Loubressac, rejoin the GR 480-652 heading west through the hamlet of la Poujade. The Gouffre de Padirac can be reached by leaving the GR, taking the D14 SW at a crossroads. Otherwise continue along a minor road for about 3 km when the path branches off right along a track and then left along a path, passing some ruins to the right. From here the path descends steeply towards the Dordogne, crossing the Gintrac road at the tiny settlement of Taillefer where walkers who detour to the Gouffre de Padirac would probably rejoin the path. The route descends left, overlooking the Dordogne, before looping back uphill to reach the hamlet of Magnagues. The path descends again, crosses the D3 and reaches the riverside village of Carennac.*

Carennac is a beautiful Quercy village replete with 16th century golden stone houses and turreted manor-houses clustering around the priory and church of St Pierre. The priory, which was damaged in the Revolution, still retains its fortified gateway and a hexagonal priory tower. The Romanesque church, next to the castle, is noted for its superb 12th century carved tympanum and its restored two-storey cloisters. The writer and churchman Fénelon is supposed to have written his masterpiece, *Télémaque*, at Carennac where he spent 15 years as senior prior.

DAY FIVE - CARENNAC TO ROCAMADOUR (24 KM; 6 HRS)

Variety is a keynote of the final day's walk which initially wends high above the Dordogne to the spectacular Cirque de Montvalent before heading inland over the remote expanses of the Gramat Causse towards the amazing site of Rocamadour on the cliff face of the Alzou gorge.

The GR 480-652 path climbs out of Carennac NW, high above the course of the Dordogne for several kilometres, providing filtered views of the river. It contours around a gentle bend in the river and then climbs up to a farm where you turn left onto a lane, following it south through woodland. The route leaves the lane right (W) and soon joins another to cross a minor road. The path enters more woods, descends a gully, skirts left around the village of Floirac and crosses the Floirac road. A detour into Floirac for lunch provisions is easily made. The walk can be substantially shortened to allow an afternoon exploration of Rocamadour by catching the train from the Floirac train halt to the Rocamadour-Padirac station. Soon the path turns sharply south and climbs up to the causse cliffs of the Cirque de Montvalent, affording picturesque views of the valley and a cingle, a meandering loop in the Dordogne below. The path soon joins a farm track and you head SW through the settlement of Veyssou. In a further 2.5 km, mainly on farm tracks, you reach the village of Montvalent.

At Montvalent, the GR 46 is joined and followed to Rocamadour. Head south on the east side of the busy N140 road for almost 1 km. Cross the road and continue south, passing to the right of a château at la Sarladie and descending through woodland. The D15 is crossed and the path climbs again, joining a minor road SW for 1 km when you turn right to follow a farm track to the buildings of les Alis. Turn left onto a minor road which leads, after 1 km, into the hamlet of l'Hospitalet where there are excellent views of the Alzou gorge and Rocamadour, less than 2 km away. The route now follows the 'holy road' used by pilgrims,

Rocamadour, true to its name, embraces the rock face high above the river Alzou.

passing near l'Hospitalet's 13th century chapel and the ruins of the pilgrim hospital, then under the Porte de l'hopital *before joining the D32 road and entering* Rocamadour *through the* Porte du Figuier *or 'fig tree gate'.*

One of the most famous pilgrimage centres from the 12th to 14th centuries, Rocamadour is still a shrine and a well-touristed village best seen out of season or late in the day when the coaches have departed. Inside its gates, houses and souvenir shops line its single pedestrian street, above which rise the buildings of the ecclesiastical city, accessed by climbing the 223 steps of the Grand Escalier. The whole site is crowned by a château and ramparts from where there are panoramic views over the roofs of the churches and houses below. From the Grand Escalier you enter the churches' parvis, the Place St-Amadour, around which are grouped the seven churches of the ecclesiastical city. Of these, the most hallowed shrine is the Chapelle Notre-Dame containing the 12th century Black Madonna, a wooden reliquary statue which is an object of great veneration. Rocamadour, with its rich history and spectacular setting, is a fitting end to our walk.

NOTES ON THE DORDOGNE

TYPE OF WALK	One way
LENGTH OF WALK	116.5 kilometres (72 miles); five days
DIFFICULTY	An easy to medium grade, with fairly long days
START	Martel, an agricultural town on the Martel Causse
FINISH	Rocamadour, a pilgrimage site perched high above the Alzou gorge

PUBLIC TRANSPORT
SNCF train to St Denis-pres-Martel from Toulouse or Brive (or SNCF rail bus from Souillac) then SNCF rail bus 7 km to Martel. To return to St Denis-pres-Martel, take a taxi (Tel: 05) 65337227) for the 3 km trip to Rocamadour-Padirac station and catch the SNCF train from there.

LUGGAGE
Leave excess luggage at the SNCF railway station in St Denis-pres-Martel, or in Brive or Toulouse.

CLIMATE
The region enjoys a Mediterranean climate with hot summers and crisp, mild winters (although January and February can be wet and cold). Late spring and early autumn are perhaps the best times to walk.

MAP
Institut Geographique National (IGN) Serie Verte No. 48 *Périgueux Tulle* 1:100,000

PATH   Mostly on waymarked *grandes randonnées*, long-distance walking paths; some minor roads.

SHORTER VARIANT (see Days 4 & 5)
A two-day version: *Train from Brive to Biars-sur-Cere, near Bretenoux;* 1 - walk from Bretenoux to Carennac; 2 - walk from Carennac to Rocamadour; *taxi to Rocamadour-Padirac station and train to Brive.*

VILLAGES
Martel (population 1400), Turenne (700), **Collonges-la-Rouge** (400), Curemonte (200), **Beaulieu-sur-Dordogne** (1600), Gagnac-sur-Cère (700), Cornac (400), **Bretenoux** (1200), Autoire (200), Loubressac (400), **Carennac** (400), Floirac (300), Montvalent (200), **Rocamadour** (800).

ACCOMMODATION
Inexpensive hotels at each of the suggested overnight stops. Limited accommodation at Collonges and Carennac where reservations are advisable; Rocamadour can be booked out in peak summer period.

CUISINE
The Dordogne, a centre of a rich and varied regional cuisine, is a gastronome's delight. Ducks and geese are raised for *foies gras* (served as a *pâté*, *terrine* or *mousse* or included in a *ballottine*) and for *confits*, pieces of meat cooked and preserved in their fat. Perigord truffles are considered to be France's finest and they flavour many local dishes, as do such wild mushrooms as *cèpes*, *chanterelles* and *morilles*. Walnuts also feature: as oil to dress salads, in cake which is a regional speciality and in the aperitif *Quercy Noix*. *Cabecou* is a flavoursome local goats cheese often sold *sec* (dry) in shops and markets.

WILDLIFE
The farming and hunting practices of the region have left little in the way of wildlife. However, the birdlife is quite prolific and wildflowers flourish on the causses.

SPECIAL FEATURES
The medieval hilltown of Turenne; the red sandstone village of Collonges-la-Rouge; the Dordogne river; Castelnau-Bretenoux Castle; Autoire and its gorge; a detour to the Gouffre de Padirac; Carennac and its Romanesque church; Rocamadour and its ecclesiastical city.

FURTHER READING

THREE RIVERS OF FRANCE: DORDOGNE, LOT, TARN
by Freda White, photographs by Michelle Buselle, published in 1996.

DORDOGNE: PERIGORD-QUERCY
Michelin Green Guide, published by Michelin.

USEFUL ADDRESSES

OFFICE DE TOURISME
46500 Rocamadour; Tel: 05) 65 33 62 59 Fax: 05) 65 33 74 14 Email: rocamadour@wanadoo.fr

WAY OF ST JACQUES

A historic pilgrimage route through France's Massif Central, crossing the remote Aubrac plateau then descending to the beautiful Lot valley and the medieval village of Conques with its stunning Romanesque abbey.

In medieval Christendom, the shrine of Santiago de Compostela (St Jacques to the French; St James in English) in northwest Spain was a pilgrimage centre ranked third in importance behind Jerusalem and Rome's St Peters. Pilgrimages to Santiago reached their apogee in the 12th century when over half a million pilgrims flocked there each year from all over Europe. Four great pilgrim routes (beginning in Paris, Vezelay, Le Puy and Arles respectively) were used to cross France from east to west and hence into Spain over the Pyrénées. The first recorded pilgrimage to Santiago was made in 951 AD by Bishop Gottschalk from Le Puy, along a route which became known as the Via Podiensis. The four routes were described by a 12th century monk, Aimery Picaud, in a book which could be considered the world's first tourist guide. Churches, reliquary-shrines and hospices sprang up along the pilgrim routes and some of the greatest examples of Romanesque architecture can be found in villages and towns through which the routes pass.

One of France's longest *grandes randonnées* or long distance footpaths, the GR65 Chemin de St Jacques, now follows the ancient Via Podiensis fairly faithfully. Its entire 800 km length from Le Puy in the Auvergne to the Spanish town of Roncesvalles in the Pyrénées can be walked with minimal incursion from motorways and urban sprawl. Some stretches have more to offer the walker than others and the six day itinerary between Aumont-Aubrac and Conques described below provides a superb meld of remote countryside and historic interest. If time is available, you could extend the itinerary by commencing from the spectacular town of Le Puy-en-Velay, from which it is a four day walk to Aumont-Aubrac.

Our route is through the southern part of the Massif Central, France's huge central upland. It passes through two administrative *départements*: Lozère (France's least populous département) and Aveyron which roughly matches the ancient province of Rouergue. Topographically, our route begins on the Aubrac plateau: sparsely populated country now given over to pasture. The rolling hills, once forested, are now almost treeless and life in this

Christ sits in majesty on the church tympanum at Conques, the destination of this pilgrimage walk.

isolated area is no doubt hard. After crossing the Aubrac, our route descends rapidly to the valley of the river Lot which we cross at the town of St-Côme-d'Olt (the Lot was called the Olt in the local Occitan language). The descent to the deep valleys of the Lot marks the change to a far more fertile landscape, pastureland giving way to crop farming and a noticeable increase in prosperity. Our route follows the Lot for several days before parting company with it just past Estaing and heading towards Conques.

Signs of the Via Podiensis are frequently seen along the way, whether they be beautiful Romanesque chapels, carved stone crosses, or simply the scallop shell which was the badge of the St James pilgrim. Reaching the jewel of Conques is a wonderful reward for all who tread this path.

Day One - Aumont-Aubrac to Nasbinals (26 km; 7 hrs)

Our route begins in Aumont-Aubrac, a small town—probably of Roman origin—lying on the Agrippan Way (now part of the D987 road) which linked Lyon and Toulouse. For the modern traveller, Aumont-Aubrac is conveniently served by both the railway (from Clermont-Ferrand) and the A75 Paris to Béziers motorway. The church of St Etienne is a remnant of a 12th century priory and within the old town there are some well-preserved 16th and 17th century houses.

Leave Aumont early and bring lunch supplies, as the walk to Nasbinals is long with nowhere to dine en route. *Leave the town to the west via the D987 and turn left after passing under the railway line. A GR65 signpost indicates the direction and time to Nasbinals. The GR65 is well waymarked but you should keep alert for the horizontal red and white stripes on trees, telephone posts, buildings and rocks. For the next few kilometres, the GR65 path is shared with the circular GR Sentier du Pays Tour de l'Aubrac.*

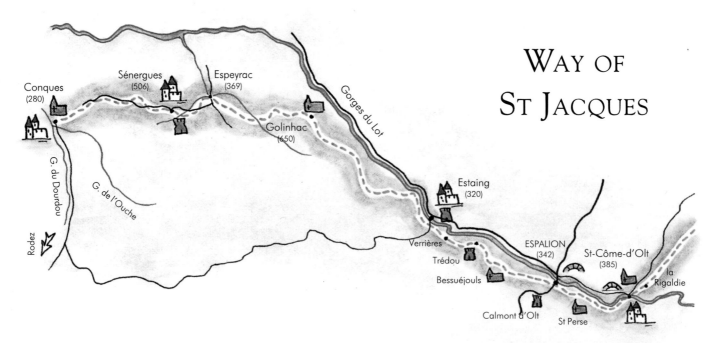

WAY OF
ST JACQUES

Turn right on a path leading uphill through woods, then join a minor road which is followed right for 400 metres. A tunnel passes beneath the A75 motorway which is too new to be marked on older maps. The path then branches left off the road and continues through woodland for 2 km. Fork right and in 500 m join a minor road (our route diverges here from the GR Tour de l'Aubrac) and continue for 1 km to the hamlet of La Chaze-de-Peyre, its church steeple visible from afar. From here the path follows a minor road for 1 km to join the D987 at the Chapelle de Bastide and leads through Lasbros after a further kilometre. Five minutes later the GR65 branches left from the D987, descends to cross a stream, bears right for 300 m and then left. In 2.5 km, having crossed the Riou Frech, a typical Aubrac granite stream, the path ascends to Le Quatre Chemins where there is a café. Here the way rejoins the D987 briefly before again forking left on a path through pine forest. It crosses the boggy Rau de la Planette and continues over open country, crossing a minor road after almost 2 km. A short diversion down this road to a bridge and the derelict Moulin de la Folle (watermill of the mad woman) provides a tranquil picnic spot by the brook.

Back on the track, notice the old *buron* uphill on the left: it is typical of rural Aubrac architecture. Burons are huts built of lava and granite, roofed with *lauzes* (limestone slabs), usually built into the slope with a single opening. They are found in the middle of pasture near a stream and were used (some still are) by cowherds as summer living quarters where they could make and mature cheese. *The track follows the course of the river Rimeize, crosses over a tributary on a granite slab bridge and passes a roadside cross at*

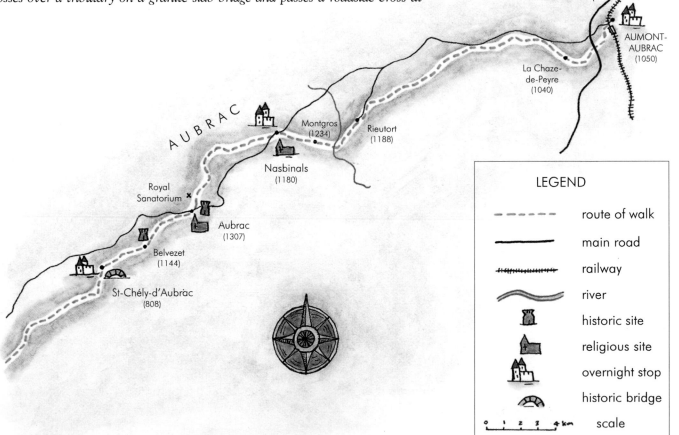

LEGEND

route of walk

main road

railway

river

historic site

religious site

overnight stop

historic bridge

scale

Ferluc before crossing the D73 road. Here the path becomes a minor road leading to the hamlet of Finieyrols (note the beautiful barn) from where the way forks right and crosses a treeless plateau, the Montagnes d'Aubrac, where dry stone walls divide fields strewn with granite boulders. The views here of rolling hills are vast and strangely beautiful. The route joins a minor road which bridges the stream of La Peyrade, and after 1 km comes to the hamlet of Rieutort-d'Aubrac. Look out for the two old fountain troughs and the communal oven before leaving the hamlet by the more westerly of the two lanes (ignore the GR65A variant which also leaves Rieutort, on a more southerly route to the town of Aubrac).

Along the way stand many beautiful roadside crosses, such as this one at Golinhac.

Our route continues SW on a minor road with views down to the river Bès on the right. A ruined watermill by the river is named on the map as Bouquincan, a corruption of Buckingham. This location may mark the defeat of the famous English captain in the 14th century. *The D900 is reached and followed right bridging the river Bès after which an uphill path is taken right to reach the hamlet of Montgros after 1.5 km. For the next 2 km, you follow a wide, stony* draille. Drailles are centuries old drove roads or trails used for the transhumance, the annual movement of cattle between the valleys and their mountain summer pasture. *The draille road descends to rejoin the D900 into Nasbinals.* Nasbinals is a market town and ski centre and prides itself on its magnificent 11th century Romanesque church. Built of local brown basalt and roofed with schist, it has an aisleless nave and octagonal bell tower and its southern porch is supported by four fine capitals, one of which depicts a battle between archer and lancer.

DAY TWO - NASBINALS TO ST-CHÉLY-D'AUBRAC (17 KM; 4.5 HRS)

Today's journey, though considerably shorter than yesterday's, is if anything wilder and more exhilarating. Lunch can be obtained in Aubrac, some 9 km from Nasbinals. *The route follows the D987 southwest out of Nasbinals and after 500 m at Le Coustat the path bears off right. After about 2 km the Chamboulies stream is crossed. Beyond this, the path bears right over open pasture, by which time the path has become a draille. It can be difficult to follow the waymarking in this area. The draille climbs gently towards Ginestouse Bas Buron (1303 m) and after a further 1 km it skirts north of a small pocket of woodland passing beneath Ginestouse Haut Buron and swings SE to the west of Ginestouse farm. Hereabouts the path leaves the département of Lozère and enters Aveyron. Near the Royal Ancient Sanatorium, the draille descends to the D987 which is followed into the village of Aubrac.*

Aubrac is the location of the annual Fête de Transhumance held on the last Sunday of May; at this time the Salers cattle are collected from the Lot valley, garlanded and moved up to the mountain meadows via the drailles. The Aubrac herders hire the cows from their owners for the summer to make cheese. Aubrac is overlooked by the Tour des Anglais which was constructed in 1353 as a defence against the English during the Hundred Years War; it now houses the gîte d'etape. Aubrac's church, built in 1220, is transitional between the Romanesque and the Gothic. These buildings and a forester's lodge once belonged to the Brothers Hospitaller of Aubrac, monastic knights who offered escort, protection and refuge to pilgrims.

The church bell was rung in stormy weather to guide lost souls to Aubrac.

Leave Aubrac by the D987 and after 500 m turn left and descend through woodland on a path. Cross a fast-flowing mountain stream and pick up a wider draille which continues to descend towards Belvezet. Before reaching Belvezet, diverge left from the draille and follow a path around a basalt outcrop on which is perched the ruins of a Templars castle dominating the hamlet below. From Belvezet, descend on woodland paths then turn left onto a minor road near ruins. Follow the road for 1 km down to the village of St-Chély-d'Aubrac, snug in its picturesque valley setting.

Day Three - St-Chély to St-Côme-d'Olt (16 km; 4 hrs)

Today, you complete the descent from the Aubrac plateau, passing through a succession of beautiful landscapes down to the fertile and picturesque Lot valley. Take lunch supplies unless you plan to arrive at St-Côme by lunch time. *The route leaves St-Chély to the south, crossing the Boralde de St-Chély on a minor road over an old bridge on which there is a 16th century Calvary cross, decorated with a pilgrim holding his staff and rosary. At this point the GR6, which entered St-Chély from another direction, diverges left. Your GR65 route climbs to the right, behind the cemetery, joins the D19 and then veers right onto a minor road passing through the hamlet of Le Recours. After this you descend right on a path through oak forest and after 2 km reach Les*

Isolated burons relieve the bleak expanse of the Aubrac plateau.

St-Côme, with its unusual twisted church spire, nestles above the river Lot.

Cambrassats. Turn left onto a minor road contouring around a hill. Pass Foyt and ignore the Bessiere turn off at 1.5 km, but then turn right soon after towards L'Estrade.

The route diverges right just before entering L'Estrade and follows a path westwards through chestnut woods before crossing a road and descending to ford a stream. The path then ascends to a minor road which soon joins the D557. Cross this and take a path along the left bank of the Boralde stream. Cross an old bridge and rejoin the D557 which is followed for about 2 km into the hamlet of Martillergues. The route turns left after the last house and continues through fields. At a T-junction turn left then right on a farm road into La Rigaldie. At the communal bread oven (now a henhouse) turn left onto a path and then right, following a minor road into St-Côme-d'Olt.

St-Côme-d'Olt is classified as one of the *les plus beaux villages de France* and it is superbly situated above the river Lot. The town now spreads beyond its fortified curtain walls within which 15th and 16th century houses line the narrow lanes. The Gothic-Flamboyant style church, dedicated to St Côme and St Damien, was built in 1522 by Antoine Salvanh. It is famed for its unusual twisted belltower and ornate studded Renaissance doors. The present town hall is an 11th century château, once home to the lords of Calmont and Castenau. Outside the town walls are some elegant Renaissance houses and the 11th century Chapelle des Pénitents, a beautifully proportioned Romanesque chapel which was St-Côme's first church.

DAY FOUR - ST-CÔME-D'OLT TO ESTAING (17 KM; 4.75 HRS)

Today's journey, though not overly long, is so full of interesting diversions that an early start should be made. There are plenty of lunch options in Espalion (6 km from St-Côme), the largest town on the route. Our route follows above the south bank of the Lot, descending to the bustling river town of Espalion before again climbing above the Lot and following its course to the beautiful village of Estaing.

The GR6 rejoins the GR65 at St-Côme and both routes leave by the bridge at the SE edge of the town. Cross the Lot, which marks the boundary between the Aubrac and the ancient province of Rouergue. Turn right onto a riverside road for 1.5 km where the GR6 and the GR65 again diverge. Our route branches left off the road on a path steeply uphill and passes through beech, oak and chestnut woodland. After climbing to a ridge, the path veers NW, passing through private property. After about 2.5 km (at a spot height of 483 m on the map) views across the Lot valley open up. For even better views, watch carefully for a right branching path a few hundred metres further on. This leads after less than 500 m to a rock outcrop on which a large 19th century statue of the Virgin, the Vierge du Pic de Vermus, has been erected. From here there are commanding views of the valley back to St-Côme and downstream to Espalion. *Back on the main path, descend to the superb Église de Perse which deserves close inspection.* Built in the 11th and 12th centuries and dedicated to Charlemagne's confessor, St Hilarian, this red sandstone Romanesque church was one of the daughter-houses of Conques abbey. The austere interior houses capitals sculpted with intriguing scenes such as a lion hunt. A tympanum over the main entrance depicts Pentecost above the Last Judgement. Note also the charming naive carvings of the Magi in adoration, above to the left of the portal. *The GR6 rejoins the GR65 here and both follow minor roads for 1 km into Espalion.*

Espalion is full of interest. From the southern river bank, beautiful views are gained of the turreted Vieux Palais (dating from 1572 and formerly the residence of the governors of Espalion), the 11th century Pont Vieux and the old tanneries, timber-balconied buildings which line the northern bank,

Morning mist envelops the medieval bridge at Espalion.

now used as housing. The bridge is still used to herd cattle and sheep across the Lot during the transhumance. The folkloric Musée Joseph-Vaylet is housed in the restored 1472 church of St Jean and adjacent buildings. The Musée du Rouergue (local life, customs and costumes) occupies the nearby cells of the old prison. High above Espalion (3.5 km by road) on a basalt outcrop, stands the ruined medieval fortress, the Château de Calmont d'Olt, which now houses a siege museum (open in summer). The steep walk is worthwhile if time permits and there are fine views from the ruins.

The route leaves Espalion by the Rue Camille Violand running west along the southern bank of the Lot. After a somewhat suburban and dull 1.5 km, join the D556 and follow it for 1 km. Take a path left which leads, after 500 m, to the church of St Pierre-de-Bessuéjouls, nestled at the foot of a wooded hillside. Unpretentious on the outside and at first sight inside, this 16th century church hides an extraordinary little Romanesque chapel beneath its 11th century belltower (a vestige from an earlier church), reached by a worn and narrow stone staircase which ascends from a rear corner. This chapel of pink sandstone is exquisitely decorated with archaic motifs including knotwork and Maltese crosses on sculpted capitals inspired by those at Conques abbey. Note also the 9th century altar, carved with Archangels and St Michael slaying the dragon.

Continue on a minor road, cross a stream and then climb NW on a steep path to a plateau before joining another minor road which passes through the hamlet of Griffoul. In a few minutes, the route diverges right onto a dirt track and descends gradually to pass the Château of Beauregard and the church of Trédou. From here, backroads are followed for 3 km into the beautiful and well-preserved village of Verrières. Take the D556 and then follow the D100 along the bank of the Lot. After 500 m, diverge left off the D100 and climb through forest before descending and rejoining the road which crosses the Gothic bridge into the classified village of Estaing.

Estaing is a delightfully picturesque medieval village. The houses of the old town huddle around the 15th century château and church of St Fleuret. Notice the magnificent sculpted stone cross outside the church's south doorway depicting a kneeling pilgrim. The château was once the home of the Comtes d'Estaing but is now a convent which may be visited: the views over the town from the high dungeon tower are dramatic. If time permits, visit the Chapelle de l'Ouradou (1.5 km north on the D97); this small chapel dating from 1529 is now surrounded by farm buildings.

DAY FIVE - ESTAING TO SÉNERGUES (26 KM; 7.25 HRS)

Today's journey is again a long one and Golinhac, 15 km from Estaing, is the only village where lunch may be purchased. Note that the GR65 has only recently been rerouted to pass through Sénergues; the map may show it passing to the north. *Cross the bridge and turn right onto a minor road which is followed for 3 km, where the GR65 diverges left before the hamlet of La Rouquette. After 750 m, cross a bridge over the Ruisseau de Luzane and take a forest path which short-cuts the hairpin bends of a climbing road and reaches*

Light streams into the exquisite chapel at St Pierre-de-Bessuéjouls.

The slate-roofed houses of Estaing, viewed from the château's high dungeon tower.

Montegut. *The route continues to climb and alternate between forest path and road until, at spot height 464 m, a minor road is followed through woodland then farmland to the hamlet of Le Mas. After some bends in the road, the route follows a path left before the hamlet of Falguières. Massip is reached after 2 km of woodland paths and Golinhac is reached after a further 1.5 km of paths and minor roads.* Golinhac commands fine views of the surrounding country-side. The church of St Martin has a beautiful altar and the village boasts an ancient stone cross, its base decorated with a pilgrim bearing a staff.

A path from behind the church leads west through fields to Le Poteau and at a junction continues west on the D42 then WNW on a path to Les Albusquiès after which you follow minor roads and farm paths into the hamlet of Campagnac where the GR6 rejoins the GR65. A winding road descends through farm and woodland through the hamlets of Le Soulie and Carboniès into the village of Espeyrac on the river Daze. Note the old stone cross at the entrance to the village. Espeyrac has a hotel-restaurant and a shop and offers an alternative overnight stop to nearby Sénergues. *From Espeyrac, a footbridge crosses the river by the cemetery and a minor road is followed. After about 500 m, watch for a road branching left; the GR65 has been rerouted from this point for several kms. Join the D42 briefly before branching left on a minor road to Sénergues.* This pretty village, with its partly restored château, has hotels which may be closed out of season. It is also serviced by buses to Conques.

High above the river Lot, the path heads over rich farming land towards the remote village of Conques.

DAY SIX - SÉNERGUES TO CONQUES (10 KM; 3 HRS)

Today's short journey allows you to reach Conques by midday, leaving maximum time to explore the village and see the church. *From Sénergues, follow the D42 briefly SW then diverge right uphill on a minor road and a path bordering a forest. The path glances the D42, then rejoins it nearly 2 km further on, just before a junction with the D137 where you take another minor road through farmland. After 500 m, turn west to rejoin the D42 which is followed into Fontromieu. Take a minor road to the hamlet of St-Marcel and, 1.5 km further on, pick up a steep, stony path which branches left and descends into Conques.*

Built above the confluence of two rivers, Conques is an unashamedly beautiful medieval village whose golden stone houses range up the hillside on narrow zigzagging lanes clustering around the magnificent former abbey church of Ste Foy. Conques is full of hotels, restaurants and shops with many artisans and artists working there. The village is host to concerts in July and August and on the second Sunday in October there is a pilgrimage procession. A good vantage point for viewing the village and church is the Chapelle St-Roch, reached from the rue Charlemagne.

Conques, once simply a halt on the pilgrimage route, became a pilgrimage destination in its own right in the 9th century when it acquired the relics of the 4th century child martyr, Ste Foy (or St Faith). Legend has it that a monk from the poor abbey of Conques insinuated himself into the wealthy abbey at Agen and was eventually entrusted with guarding the relics which he promptly purloined. As a result of this 'holy theft', Conques' treasury now holds arguably the most important collection of medieval and Renaissance goldwork in Western Europe. The Romanesque church, completed in the 12th century, was built on the site of an earlier Carolingian church and fell into disuse when pilgrim numbers dwindled. It was reduced to ruins during the wars of religion and, near collapse, was saved from destruction in the 19th century when the two towers were rebuilt.

Conques' abbey church of
Ste Foy, the goal of pilgrims
for many centuries.

The simple, elegant interior soars to a height of 22 metres with a nave comprised of three tiers of arches topped by over 200 decorated capitals (binoculars are useful). The wide chancel allowed numerous pilgrims to file past the saint's relics once displayed there; these are now exhibited in the Treasury. The tympanum above the west doorway depicting the Last Judgement is one of the glories of Romanesque sculpture in its mastery, originality and dimensions. Originally polychrome, it is remarkably preserved, having been resited from the church's interior in the 16th century. Ideally it should be viewed, with the aid of binoculars and an interpretive guide, in the late afternoon when the crowds have thinned and the sunlight works its magic on the stone.

NOTES ON WAY OF ST JACQUES

TYPE OF WALK   One way

LENGTH OF WALK   114 kilometres (72 miles); six days. To lengthen, start at Le Puy.

DIFFICULTY   A medium grade walk, with two long days

START   Aumont-Aubrac, high on the remote Aubrac plateau

FINISH   Conques, a historic village above the Ouche and Dourdon gorges

PUBLIC TRANSPORT
Train or SNCF rail bus from Clermont-Ferrand to Aumont-Aubrac. From Conques, take the early morning bus to Rodez (no Sunday service). To return to Aumont-Aubrac, then take an SNCF rail bus from Rodez to Severac-le-Chateau and a train to Aumont-Aubrac.

LUGGAGE   Leave excess luggage at Aumont-Aubrac SNCF railway station.

CLIMATE
Snow covers the Aubrac plateau in winter and can fall from late October onwards. All facilities should be open from June to September. Late spring and early autumn are the best times to walk. Major temperature changes (20°C is not unusual) can be experienced during the course of a day.

MAP   Institut Géographique National (IGN) 1:100,000 *serie verte* No. 58 Rodez - Mende

PATH
The entire route is on the waymarked GR 65, an official French long-distance path following an ancient pilgrimage trail. The route includes footpaths, woodland tracks and minor country roads.

SHORTER VARIANT   (see Days 4, 5 & 6)
A three-day version: *Train to Rodez and bus to Espalion;* 1 - walk from Espalion to Estaing;
2 - walk from Estaing to Espeyrac or Senergues; 3 - walk to Conques; *bus from Conques to Rodez.*

VILLAGES
Aumont-Aubrac (population 950), **Nasbinals** (550), Aubrac (150), **St-Chély-d'Aubrac** (580), **St-Côme-d'Olt** (850), Espalion (4,600), **Estaing** (650), Espeyrac (280), **Sénergues** (650), **Conques** (360).

ACCOMMODATION
Most of the villages and towns have a gîte d'etape (self catering hostels for walkers), as well as several simple hotels. Of the overnight stops, Sénergues has the fewest hotels.

CUISINE
The Auvergne is renowned for its cheeses: Roquefort, St-Nectaire, Cantal, bleu d'Auvergne and Fourme d'Ambert are just a few. Salt pork with Le Puy lentils and *falette* (stuffed breast of veal) are both Auvergne specialities. Other regional dishes include *aligot* (a concoction with mashed potato, tomme cheese and garlic), *choux forcis* (cabbage stuffed with veal mince) and *cassoulet* (a slow-cooked dish with various meats and vegetables). Mushrooms are plentiful in autumn and fish abound in the streams and rivers. This area is not known for its wine, although some is produced near Estaing.

WILDLIFE
Raptors are a common sight on the Aubrac. Wildflowers such as sawwort, pansy and gentian abound in spring; in autumn the mushrooms are an amazing sight. Woods of chestnut, walnut and beech trees.

SPECIAL FEATURES
The moorlands of the Aubrac plateau; Romanesque churches and chapels such as St Perse and Bessuéjouls; the medieval villages of St-Côme-d'Olt, Estaing and Conques; the Romanesque abbey church of Ste Foy and its treasures at Conques.

FURTHER READING

THE WAY OF SAINT JAMES: THE GR65
by Hal Bishop, published by Cicerone Press, 1989

THE WAY OF SAINT JAMES: PILGRIM ROADS TO SANTIAGO DE COMPOSTELA
by T.A.Layton, published 1976

MICHELIN GREEN GUIDE: PYRÉNÉES/LANGUEDOC/TARN GORGES
published by Michelin, 1996

USEFUL ADDRESSES

CONFRATERNITY OF ST JAMES
57 Leopold Road, London N2 8BG

COMITE REGIONAL DU TOURISME (MIDI-PYRÉNÉES)
3 Rue de l'Esquile, 31000 Toulouse, Tel: (61) 23 2205

COMITE REGIONAL DU TOURISME (AUVERGNE)
45 Avenue Julien, 63000 Clermont-Ferrand, Tel: (73) 93 040

THE VERDON GORGE

A demanding but unforgettable excursion combining the rugged scenery of Haute Provence's limestone mountains with a descent through Europe's deepest gorge, the spectacular Grand Canyon du Verdon.

For millions of tourists who flock there annually, Provence conjures up images of the glamorous and often gaudy stretch of the Mediterranean coastline beloved of wealthy hedonists. Inland from this beckons the real Provence, sharing in the sunshine and famed Provençal light and embracing wild and dramatic landscapes on a truly grand scale. Much of inland Provence is heavily forested and mountainous, comprising several ranges of limestone *préalpes* (alpine foothills). The *Préalpes de Castellane* have been eroded along a geological fault line by the river Verdon to form a gorge over 700 m deep in parts of its 21-km length. This awesome gorge was an all but impenetrable barrier between north and south before the capricious Verdon was tamed for hydroelectric power. It was only fully explored in 1905 by speleologist Edouard Martel and the vertiginous north-bank road was not completed until 1973. Now known as an outdoor enthusiast's paradise, the spectacular Grand Canyon du Verdon justly attracts walkers, climbers, canyonists, rafters and kayakers alike during summer. In 1997 the *Parc Naturel Régional du Verdon* was chartered to safeguard this extraordinary natural site. For the walker, its beauty can be enjoyed on waymarked paths which descend to the river on both sides of the gorge. Far less frequented is the wild mountain scenery in the remote country to the east of the Verdon, between Entrevaux and Castellane. This is a depopulated area where, sadly, walkers' refuges have closed in recent years for lack of patronage.

The five-day walk described here follows a section of the 1100-km-long GR4, one of France's first and longest *grandes randonnées* and provides some of the most singular walking in the south of France. Our walk commences in the upper Var river valley at the fortified village of Entrevaux from where it climbs steeply to become a remote ridge walk (a *crête* is a ridge) traversing the wooded mountains between the rivers Var and Verdon. The tiny settlements, ruined chapels and farm buildings encountered en route serve as a reminder of the region's population decline. The way descends to the Verdon at the thriving town of Castellane and climbs again, eschewing the road which hugs the Verdon to traverse the twisted limestone formations of the mountains north of the river and the ancient perched villages

The green waters of the river Verdon swirl through the Grand Canyon du Verdon.

38

THE VERDON GORGE

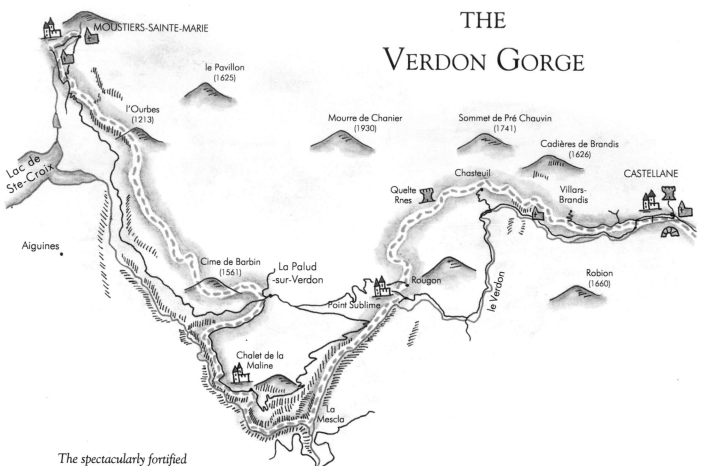

The spectacularly fortified town of Entrevaux on the Var.

high above the valley. After descending to Rougon, the first sight of the main gorge is truly memorable as is the fourth day's walk through the gorge on the famous *Sentier Martel*, a footpath which has been hewn out of the rock face in a triumph of engineering. On the last day the path climbs once more to gain further prospects of the mighty gorge and of the artificial Lac de Sainte-Croix into which the Verdon flows. After a final descent you reach your destination, the delightful Moustiers-Sainte-Marie, a golden-hued village cleft in two by a torrent and backed by limestone cliffs.

Though not technically difficult, this walk is nonetheless challenging. A long first day, involving much height gain and a detour off the GR4 to tiny Soleilhas is necessitated by the lack of accommodation on the path between Entrevaux and Castellane. Subsequent days, though shorter, also involve considerable height variations and the walk along the Sentier Martel negotiates several long tunnels (carry a torch) and steep metal ladders. These rigours are a small price to pay for the chance to encounter such magnificent scenery.

DAY ONE - ENTREVAUX TO SOLEILHAS (25.5 KM; 9 HRS)

The walk begins at medieval Entrevaux, a 90-minute journey from Nice on

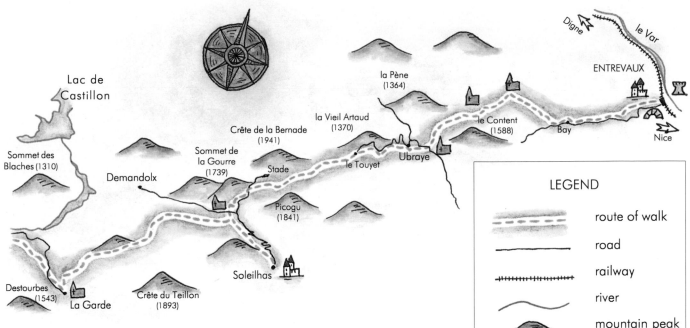

LEGEND

	route of walk
	road
	railway
	river
	mountain peak
	cliff walls
	overnight stop
	chapel
	bridge / ruins
	scale

the wonderful *Train des Pignes*. Travelling on this narrow-gauge railway line is a scenic expedition in itself, superb mountain vistas opening up as it wends its way through the valley of the river Var. Entrevaux stands astride the Var beneath a triangular spur of rock upon which perches its citadel. It was once a frontier outpost on the old border between French Provence and the Duchy of Savoie. It was fortified by the famous military engineer Vaubin in 1690 against invasion by the Duke's forces. Vaubin connected the Citadel with the town via a walled walkway which zigzags up through twenty gateways. He also erected the town walls which are entered through a gated drawbridge over the river Var. Entrevaux has changed little in appearance since the 17th century and you should make the effort to walk up to the citadel to sample the remarkable views after exploring the town itself. There are no shops between Entrevaux and Soleilhas so ensure you have sufficient food and water before setting out.

Leave Entrevaux on the D610 road signposted to Bay and soon turn right passing left of a house on a narrow tiled footpath. Note that the GR waymarkings (red and white stripes) are poor until Bay. Keep straight on; do not cross the boardwalk over the little gully. Cross a minor road and then another road, continuing uphill. Turn right onto the road then right onto a vehicular track up to a Spanish-style house and continue along this track winding uphill. Soon after the track surface deteriorates, take a path forking left, climbing around and above a deserted building to meet the road where you turn right uphill. Soon turn right off the road then quickly left on a poorly waymarked path (this is also a regional trail waymarked with a mountain symbol on a small white disc) which zigzags uphill before levelling and entering attractive oak woodland where the waymarking improves. A broad vehicular track is joined and, where the track curves soon after, take a narrow footpath (easily missed) right uphill. Reach the paved road and turn right uphill, turning off right onto a parallel footpath at a house. Soon rejoin the road which is followed into Bay.

*The remote village of Ubraye
basks in the Provençal sun.*

Continue to the restored Chapelle de St Claude and after about 1 km on the paved road turn right uphill near a building onto a broad stony path. The steepish climb continues through oak wood to the tree-covered ridge top (the Travers du Content) before descending steeply through coppiced beech woodland to a clearing at the Col de St-Jeannet where there is a shrine and a junction of paths. Turn left (SW), descending less steeply; to the right are wonderful mountain views and presently an evocative view of the buildings of the Chapelle de St-Jean du Desert. Walk past a small fountain, the first water supply since Entrevaux, and over a landslide to reach a signpost where you turn sharp left, signed GR4 to Ubraye. The path skirts left of a ravine and reaches the shrine at the Col de St-Jean where you turn left downhill. At a fork in the track, keep right and look for waymarks, descending through a pretty valley to eventually reach the Chapelle Notre-Dame de la Riviere and cross a stone bridge over a stream. Now turn right onto the D10 road and after 0.5 km, cross a bridge and take the second path left. The path climbs to Ubraye, passing the village's old communal oven. After five hours of walking, the water pump at Ubraye makes a scenic spot for a late lunch.

Leave Ubraye on the road, passing the church. Shortly before the sign which marks the village limits, turn left along a vehicular track and take the gravel track right at a roadside cross. Head towards some buildings and climb steeply on a path leading up to the le Touyet road. Pause often to appreciate the exquisite prospect of Ubraye as it becomes more distant. Follow the road briefly left before again leaving it left at a hairpin and climbing steeply. This path eventually levels to skirt a mountain just beneath the road before climbing again to reach a pathside cross from where le Touyet can be seen. Continue on the path contouring around the hillside and turn left at the road. The GR4 follows the road through tiny le Touyet (where there is a public phone) and turns left onto a broad track. Pass a small shrine, continuing uphill until you reach a hairpin in the track (25 minutes from le Touyet) where you descend on a footpath left at a GR4 sign. The path leads down a picturesque gully to cross a stream before climbing steeply and then levelling as it passes beneath the peak of Picogu. The mountain scenery is dramatic hereabouts with the summits of la Bernade and la Gourre and their connecting ridge standing imposingly to the right.

The path becomes indistinct (look for waymarkings on rocks) as it climbs gradually through treeless meadows to the broad Col de Vauplane, at 1650 m the highest point reached on this walk. Head for the Stade de Neige ski complex and reach the road, following it downhill until it starts to zigzag. Look carefully for a poorly signed path off right and immediately fork left descending into a ravine. Care is required navigating here; yellow and blue waymarks are also encountered. Presently you reach the Chapelle de St Barnabe nestled in beautiful surrounds. Just below the chapel, the GR path diverts on a grassy track to the right but to detour to Soleilhas you should continue on a broad, unsurfaced track straight ahead, eventually crossing the Soleilhas road (D102) at a metal cross. Now continue downhill on a fairly steep, stony path (waymarked with orange dots) through more beautiful mountain scenery, for 2 km to reach Soleilhas. Soleilhas offers one hotel-restaurant (open all year) and a gîte d'étape.

DAY TWO - SOLEILHAS TO CASTELLANE (15 KM; 4.5 HRS)

Today's walk, much shorter than yesterday's, takes in more mountain scenery as it descends to the valley of the Verdon. You could vary and extend the day's walk by ascending le Teillon en route to la Garde. The directions below regain the GR4 and allow an afternoon to explore Castellane.

Leave Soleilhas by retracing your steps up the path to the junction with the D102 which you follow towards Castellane for 750 m to where the GR4 comes in right from the Chapelle de St Barnabe. Here at a signboard you take the waymarked track, veering left and initially following the line of the road. This broad and level forest track is followed for several km as it contours around the Crête du Teillon. You gain excellent views of Demandolx village across a ravine. Later there are views of the dams of Chaudanne and Castillon, two of the artificial lakes harnessing the Verdon for water and hydroelectricity, and superb views of the mountains beyond. On a downhill section, leave the track, veering left onto a narrow footpath through bushes. Cross a stream and return to the track, following it to emerge at the ruins of the Clot d'Agnon at a pylon. Care is required here to find the way; after descending to the second pylon where the cables change direction, a shorter GR4 variant descends to Castellane underneath the pylons whereas the main GR4 route via la Garde continues ahead, descending more gradually and soon narrowing to a footpath. This descends through woodland, providing views of le Teillon, to eventually reach the N85 (Route Napoleon) at la Garde. This tiny village, dating from the 12th century, was once guarded by a château from which it derives its name. The church of

Spanned by a medieval bridge, the Verdon passes beneath le Roc at the edge of Castellane.

*The striking formation of the
Cadières de Brandis.*

*Close by, you reach the pretty
perched village of Chasteuil.*

Notre-Dame des Ormeaux was constructed on the château's ruins. Take time to explore the village's buildings to the south of the N85.

The GR4 follows the main road out of la Garde and branches left off the road soon after passing a chapel. A narrow footpath descends to reach a track where you turn left, descending the Ravin de Destourbes and crossing a stream to join a minor road. Continue for 2 km or so, then turn left onto the N85 for a 1.5 km road walk. Leave the N85 to cross the river Verdon on the 15th century footbridge, skirting the base of a cliff to enter Castellane.

Though Castellane itself is invisible from a distance, you will have had excellent views from the GR4 of the extraordinary limestone outcrop which overlooks it. Known simply as *le Roc*, it bears the 18th century chapel of Notre-Dame-du-Roc where once there was a Roman fort. A steep path to the chapel, starting from behind the Romanesque church of St-Victor, is lined with the stations of the cross and offers wonderful views. It passes above the Tour Pentagonale and a section of the ruined 14th century fortifications, built when the inhabitants of Castellane moved down off the rock into the valley. Peaceful out of season, Castellane teems with tourists and lovers of the outdoors in the height of summer when it is wise to reserve accommodation. There is a tourist office here, along with banks and other facilities.

DAY THREE - CASTELLANE TO POINT SUBLIME (18 KM; 5.5 HRS)

On today's walk the GR4 passes through some of the finest mountain scenery in southern France en route to the Point Sublime at the head of the Grand Canyon du Verdon. Much of this route follows an ancient Roman road. Before leaving, buy food in Castellane for a picnic lunch.

Take the road from the main bridge along the north bank of the Verdon. Turn right at a T-junction and left onto the D952, soon veering right on the minor C8 road signposted to Villars-Brandis. Behind you, the receding views of Castellane beneath le Roc are worth turning to admire. Walk through the hamlet of la Colle near the end of which the GR4 leaves the C8 left over a bridge on a broad track. This track contours around a mountain, providing striking views of the river below. Note that the track which climbs to the hamlet of Villars-Brandis is marked on some maps as the main GR4 route. Since the closure of Villars' gîte, however, it has been rerouted at a lower level, passing beneath Villars and the ruins of Brandis. *The path continues to contour beneath dramatic terrain, most strikingly, the serrated cliff formations of the Cadières de Brandis silhouetted against the horizon.* The hardy hiker with 4 or more hours to spare could incorporate a worthwhile ascent of the Cadières (*chairs* in Provençal) by detouring to Villars. Also on view here are two imposing peaks which squeeze the Verdon through its first narrowing: the Pic de Taloire with its summit chapel on the opposite bank and an unnamed peak near the path on which the Chapelle St-Jean is visible. It can be reached with a 10 minute detour left about 0.5 km after the Villars-Brandis junction.

The GR4 continues toward the tiny perched village of Chasteuil, passing a right-hand path to Blieux and a water source. Chasteuil is an eye-catching cluster of golden buildings set amidst mountain scenery. It has a *buvette* and a *creperie* (both open only in summer) and *chambres d'hotes* with meals. *From here, the path climbs gradually through forest to the Col de Coron, passing to the left of the Rocher de Baux. At a ruined building a signpost directs you to veer left for Rougon. Gradually the scenery alters; you are now on the Plateau de Suech, a lonely expanse of moorland, denuded of trees, where sheep are grazed. At the far edge of the plateau there is another signed path junction: continue straight on a wide path towards pylons. Descend beneath the cables on a broad, stony path, contouring right of the Barre de Catalan. You will soon glimpse the perched village of Rougon standing sentinel over the entrance to the Grand Canyon beyond. At a small shrine a footpath diverts left steeply downhill for Rougon.* Overlooked by medieval ruins, Rougon is extremely photogenic in the late afternoon light. Though lacking accommodation it has the only shop before la Mâline. *From Rougon it is a steep 15 minute descent to the D952 where you turn left to reach the Auberge du Point Sublime, the only hotel in the vicinity.*

DAY FOUR - POINT SUBLIME TO LA MALINE (12 KM; 7 HRS)

On today's route, the GR4 follows the course of the *Sentier Martel*, the classic walk through the Grand Canyon du Verdon created by the Touring Club de France and named after the speleologist who explored it. Make sure you have food and water; a packed picnic lunch may be ordered the night before if staying at the *auberge*. River water should be purified and

Rougon, with its huddle of venerable red-tiled houses.

you will need a torch. Walkers should check weather conditions and river flow before setting out. Before commencing, it is well worth crossing the fissured limestone sheets of the Plateau des Lauves to the Point Sublime Belvédère for a splendid view of the Couloir Samson (or 'corridor') and the entrance to the Grand Canyon some 190 m below.

From the auberge, walk along the D952 towards Castellane. After 50 m the GR4 path veers sharply right downhill. Soon the GR49 forks left; continue right beneath the cliffline descending to meet the dead end D23B road at a car park. Make a short detour from here through a rock tunnel to view the torrent of le Baou as it cascades into the Verdon. Concrete steps from the car park lead across a footbridge over the Baou. After climbing more steps you reach the entrance to the Tunnel du Baou, 670 m long and 3 m in diameter, which cuts through the narrows of the Couloir Samson. There are several 'windows' along the tunnel's left wall providing views of the river below and, after about 400 m, there is access to a steep stairway down to the river at the mouth of the Baume aux Pigeons, a vast cave 20 m high at the foot of a 350 m cliff through which the river flows. The tunnel ends about 250 m after this detour and is soon followed by the much shorter Tunnel de Trescaire. After this you bypass a third tunnel and for the next few hours' walking remain within earshot and often in sight of the river, sometimes climbing to avoid natural obstacles and sometimes dropping to river level. Watch for the rock formations known as the Tours de Trescaire on the opposite bank.

The path descends to the river at a pebbly beach which makes an idyllic spot for lunch and possibly a swim. After this it soon begins a steep switchback climb to bypass a rockface, reaching 200 m above river level before gradually descending beneath impressive overhangs. The path again climbs to reach a series of metal ladders ascending the Brèche Imbert, a narrow cleft between rockface and crag. At the top of the ladders there is a wonderful viewpoint to the left. The path begins another descent and soon reaches a sign indicating the nominal halfway point of the Sentier Martel. Below here the Verdon changes direction sharply at la Mescla ('mixing' in Provençal), the confluence with the river Artuby. A side path takes you down to this beautiful spot (20 minutes return). Further on, the main path descends to the river and ascends steeply once more (via fixed cable and short ladders) and continues up and down for some time before commencing the final ascent out of the gorge.

Before this ascent you reach a signposted path junction indicating the beginning of the GR99 which descends to the river. Note that the Passerelle de l'Estellie, a footbridge over the Verdon on the GR99, was washed away in 1994 and has yet to be rebuilt: it is not possible to detour to the beautiful Sentier d'Imbut on the other side of the gorge or to climb out of the gorge on the south bank. *The GR4 climbs steeply away from the river, zigzagging up to another ladder and continuing towards the top of the cliff. The Chalet de la Mâline on the D23 road above comes into sight as the path contours around the hillside.* The chalet is superbly positioned on the rim of the gorge with breath-taking canyon views available from its terrace. If the walkers' chalet is full, you can telephone for a taxi to the village of la Palud.

The view of the gorge looking back shortly before the ascent of the Brèche Imbert.

DAY FIVE - LA MALINE TO MOUSTIERS-STE-MARIE (23.5 KM; 8 HRS)

The final day's walk follows the Route des Crêtes (D23 road) to la Palud-sur-Verdon, initially paralleling the gorge and passing a series of viewing platforms with bird's-eye views over the gorge. From la Palud, the GR4 climbs to become a ridge walk culminating in grand vistas over Lac de Sainte-Croix and the Plateau de Vallensole before a descent to Moustiers through jagged limestone rock forms. Lunch can be purchased in la Palud.

Take the D23 left from the chalet to walk the 8 km to la Palud (or alternatively telephone for a local taxi) passing the Belvédères du Baucher, du Maugue and then d'Imbut where the gorge narrows and the Verdon disappears beneath a chaos of fallen rocks. The road now leaves the gorge and climbs gradually NE towards la Palud. Once a potter's village, la Palud is now a centre catering for outdoor adventure enthusiasts. It has plenty of accommodation and food shops. *The GR4 leaves la Palud on the D123 to Châteauneuf. At an old shrine where the D123 bends, take the no-through road left and, where the road ends, take the stony footpath left uphill.* As la Palud recedes, you gain beautiful views of the surrounding farmland and the mountains beyond. As you contour around the Cime de Barbin you get final views south of the narrow fingers of the gorge. *Now in forest, you may see and hear forestry work in progress and care should be taken to avoid a wrong turn on the many forest tracks. Eventually you reach a track junction beyond which are the ruins of the Jas de Barbin. Bear left here but ignore two subsequent left-hand turns, cross a wide stony path and, shortly after, pick it up again and follow it.*

At a junction (spot height 1224 m) take the GR4 straight ahead over the Plain de Barbin to eventually reach the Col de Plein Voir (or go left over the Crêtes de Plein Voir on a longer but more scenic waymarked route to the col). A little further on, near the first of two electricity pylons, is an excellent lunch spot, commanding a superb view of the Lac de Sainte-Croix. The path now descends to pass under the second pylon and reach the Col de l'Ane, 'the pass of the donkey'. Ignore side paths, remaining on the ridge to climb the Signal de l'Ourbes, the highest point of the day's walk from which there are further splendid views. Descend to a plateau at the end of which begins the long continuous descent of the Crêtes de l'Ourbes to the D952. The zigzagging route is spectacular, offering close views of fantastic rock pinnacles and more distant views of the lake and the Valensole with possible glimpses of the Luberon and the Lure mountains. *The path crosses the D952 several times as it winds downhill, eventually following the road right for 500 m towards Moustiers, passing the Chapelle St-Pierre. Turn left onto the Chemin de Peyrengue and, soon after crossing a stream, turn right at a T-junction onto a gravel road through a meadow. The contrast between this gentle countryside and the limestone mountains just traversed is intense. At a path junction the GR4 heads sharply left, bypassing Moustiers but you cross the stream on concrete stepping stones to pick up a path marked with a yellow stripe; this soon becomes a minor road ascending to Moustiers.*

The lovely and lively little town of Moustiers-Sainte-Marie is a fitting end to the walk. It makes an astonishing sight, overlooking a fertile valley yet backed up against the bare cliffs of twin limestone mountains. The

Chappelle St-Pierre, dominated by its dramatic backdrop.

Evening light accentuates the beautiful setting of Moustiers.

waters of le Riou cascade down the ravine, bisecting the village. High above on a ledge is the twice-restored Chapelle de Notre-Dame de Beauvoir, a pilgrimage place since medieval times and built on a site of a 5th century chapel. It is approached on a steep path, lined with stations of the cross, passing through defensive doorways like those above Entrevaux. The views from the path and chapel over the roofscape of Moustiers to the Maire valley are magnificent. Above the chapel a gilded star is suspended from a 227-metre iron chain fastened to the rock on either side of the Riou gorge. This improbable feat was originally performed by a knight to fulfil a vow on his safe return from the crusades. The centrepiece of the village is the beautifully restored 12th century Notre-Dame church with its three-storey belltower in Lombard Romanesque style. During summer, Moustiers is a popular tourist destination, famed for its blue-glazed *faience* pottery, made in *ateliers* or workshops outside the village and sold in numerous shops.

Notes on the Verdon Gorge

Type of walk   One way

Length of walk   94 kilometres (58 miles); five days

Difficulty   A demanding walk with one very long day and significant height variation

Start   Entrevaux, a fortified town on the river Var

Finish   Moustiers-Sainte-Marie, an ancient town set beneath towering cliffs

Public Transport
Train (*Chemin de fer de Provence*) from Nice to Entrevaux. Return by bus (Saturday only except in summer) or by taxi from Moustiers to Castellane; daily afternoon bus service from Castellane to Nice.

Luggage   Leave excess luggage at a hotel in Nice (ask at the Tourist Office).

Climate
A Mediterranean climate, tempered by altitude. Summers can be very hot and dry with occasional thunderstorms; winter brings the cold and fierce Mistral wind. Spring and autumn are best for walking.

Map
D&R No.19 *En Haute Provence de Digne à St-Auban* 1:50,000 (recommended, but omits Entrevaux) or Institut Geographique National (IGN) Serie Verte No. 61 *Nice Barcelonette* 1:100,000

Path   The entire route follows the GR4, a waymarked *grande randonnée* or long-distance path.

Shorter Variant (see Days 3 & 4)
A two-day version: *Bus from Nice to Castellane;* 1 - walk from Castellane to Point Sublime; 2 - walk from P. Sublime through the Verdon Gorge to la Maline; *taxi (or bus from la Palud) to Castellane, bus to Nice.*

VILLAGES
Entrevaux (population 800), Ubraye (60), **Soleilhas** (60), la Garde (70), **Castellane** (1400), Chasteuil (30), Rougon/**Point Sublime** (60), **la Maline**/la Palud-sur-Verdon (150), **Moustiers-Sainte-Marie** (600).

ACCOMMODATION
Four of the suggested stops have inexpensive hotels; the CAF refuge at la Maline is dormitory accommodation (bring an inner sheet) with meals available.

CUISINE
Provencal cuisine shares much with neighbouring Italy: *pissaladiere* is an onion pizza sold in every boulangerie and *pistou* is the Provençal version of *pesto*. Local herbs–rosemary, tarragon, thymes and savoury–flavour everything from honey to the slow-cooked *daubes* of beef, boar and hare which grace most menus. Delicious pastes are made with olives and capers (*tapenade*) and anchovy (*anchoïade*) and *aïoli* is a garlic mayonnaise served with vegetables. *Cabridou* are small goat's cheeses preserved with herbs in olive oil. This region is not noted for its wines; anise flavoured *pastis* is the aperitif of choice.

WILDLIFE
Wildflowers and wild herbs abound. The walk passes through woodlands of beech, chestnut and oak. Many species of butterflies and moths are here; lizards bask in profusion. Birds of prey such as buzzards, lites and kestrels ride the thermals. The woods contain deer, hare and (rarely seen) wild boar.

SPECIAL FEATURES
The fortified town of Entrevaux; dramatic limestone mountains and rock formations such as the Cadières de Brandis; perched villages such as Ubraye, Chasteuil and Rougon; the descent of the Verdon gorge on the Sentier Martel; Moustiers-Sainte-Marie in its amazing setting.

FURTHER READING

WALKING THE FRENCH GORGES: A TRAIL THROUGH PROVENCE AND THE ARDECHE
by Alan Castle, published by Cicerone Press, 1993

CANYON DU VERDON: THE MOST BEAUTIFUL HIKES
English translation, published by Editions Aio, 1997

FRENCH ALPS: MICHELIN GREEN GUIDES
published by Michelin, 1998

USEFUL ADDRESSES

OFFICE DU TOURISME (TOURIST OFFICE)
Digne Tel: 04) 92315729; Fax: 04) 92322494; Castellane Tel: 04) 92836114; Fax: 04) 92837689

CHALET DE LA MALINE (CLUB ALPIN FRANCAIS) Tel: 04) 92773805

INTERNET SITE http://www.beyond.fr

THE SALZKAMMERGUT

A series of day rambles from picturesque Hallstatt in the heart of Austria's alpine lakes district, featuring exquisite mountain and lakeland scenery as well as a rich variety of geological and historical diversions.

Beloved of Austrian honeymooners and a cherished getaway for the citizens of Salzburg, the Salzkammergut is relatively little known elsewhere. This will surprise anyone who has visited what Emperor Franz Joseph I described as an 'earthly paradise' and been captivated by the beauty of its rugged mountains, pristine glacier lakes, forests and lush alpine meadows.

The Salzkammergut lies southeast of Salzburg and translates literally as the 'Salt Chamber Estate', a reference to the region's salt mines which once enriched the coffers of Salzburg's archbishop-princes. About 190 million years ago the region was covered by a shallow sea and, over time, salt crystallised as the sea water evaporated. During the Triassic period the salt deposits were trapped in subterranean basins by deep layers of clay, marl and lime, preventing their redissolution. With the later upthrusting of the Alps, the salt deposits came closer to the surface. The southern Salzkammergut is dominated by the 840 square kilometre Dachstein massif, crowned by the Dachstein (2995m) and the eight glaciers which flow down its flanks. The Dachstein massif provides a dramatic backdrop to the Hallstättersee, a glacial lake completely surrounded by vertiginous mountains. On its western bank lies Hallstatt, described by the travel writer Alex von Humboldt as 'the most beautiful lakeside village in the world'.

Hallstatt contains the world's oldest known salt mine with evidence of almost uninterrupted mining since 900 BC. In the mid nineteenth century Hallstatt achieved worldwide fame with the discovery of extensive burial grounds about 350 metres above Hallstatt. The town has since given its name to a period of prehistoric culture, the 'Hallstatt period' between 1000 and 500 BC corresponding to the Early Iron Age: various finds from this period can be seen in Hallstatt's Prehistoric Museum. The town's Catholic church features a somewhat bizarre charnel house containing the decorated skull bones of its more recent denizens. This whole region has now been designated by UNESCO as a World Heritage Site.

Hallstatt's beauty makes it popular with summer day trippers but its remoteness means that most sightseers have rejoined their coaches well

The picture-postcard village of Hallstatt clings to a narrow ledge between mountain and lake.

The Soleleitungsweg passes through farmland near Bad Goisern.

before nightfall. The town provides for various outdoor interests including boating, angling, diving, cycling and climbing. It also makes an ideal base for day walks; numerous paths start in Hallstatt itself and many others can be reached by public transport and mountain cable-cars. Walks 1, 2 and 3 begin in Hallstatt while Walk 4 utilises a postbus to reach nearby Gosausee. None of these walks involves strenuous altitude gains but the usual precautions and supplies should be taken in this mountainous region.

WALK ONE - THE SOLELEITUNGSWEG (19 KM; 5 HRS)

This beautiful walk above and around the Hallstättersee makes good use of the Salzbergbahn funicular to gain the required elevation and the ferry from Hallstatt station to return from the other side of the lake. Be sure to check the time of the last return ferry before setting out. *Make your way to the funicular ticket office in Hallstatt Lahn, the newer part of Hallstatt to the south of the old village, and take the funicular to the Rudolfsturm (or walk up the zigzagging Salzbergweg from the centre of Hallstatt).* This former castle was named after the first Habsberg ruler, Rudolph I. It was built in 1284 by his son as a watchtower to guard the nearby salt mine. Now a restaurant, the Rudolfsturm has a public viewing terrace which should be visited for the

THE

SALZKAMMERGUT

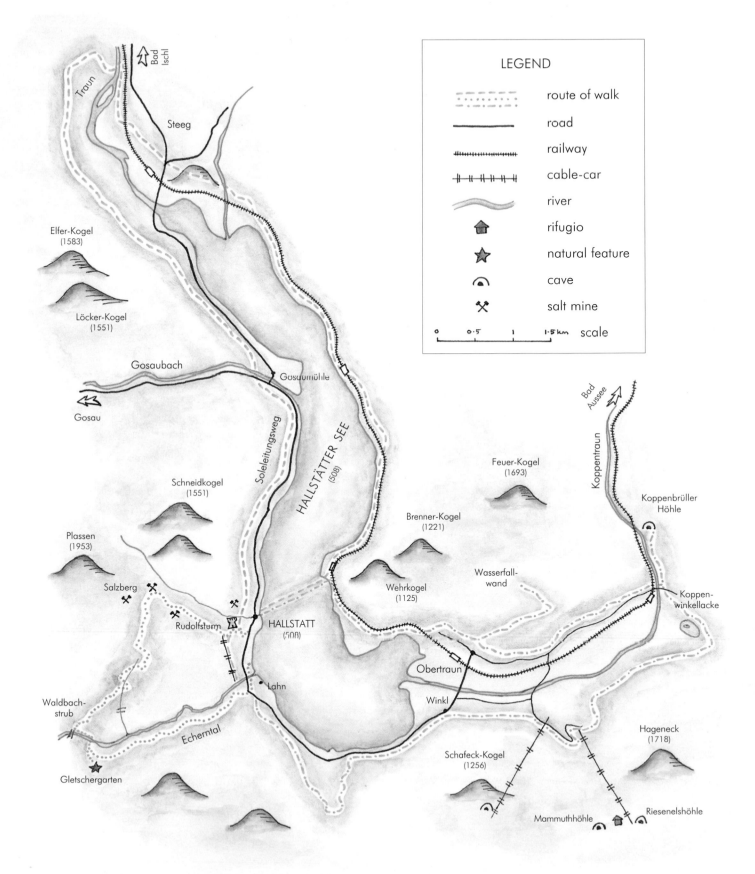

LEGEND

route of walk

road

railway

cable-car

river

rifugio

natural feature

cave

salt mine

0   0·5   1   1·5 km   scale

Bad Ischl

Traun

Steeg

Elfer-Kogel (1583)

Löcker-Kogel (1551)

Gosaubach

Gosaumühle

Gosau

Soleleitungsweg

HALLSTÄTTER SEE (508)

Bad Aussee

Koppentraun

Feuer-Kogel (1693)

Koppenbrüller Höhle

Schneidkogel (1551)

Brenner-Kogel (1221)

Plassen (1953)

Salzberg

Wehrkogel (1125)

Wasserfall-wand

Koppen-winkellacke

Rudolfsturm

HALLSTATT (508)

Lahn

Obertraun

Waldbach-strub

Winkl

Echerntal

Gletschergarten

Schafeck-Kogel (1256)

Hageneck (1718)

Mammuthhöhle

Riesenelshöhle

exquisite aerial view of Hallstatt and its lake. Higher up the valley lies the salt mine (visited in Walk 2) but our route commences immediately below the Rudolfsturm and is signposted Soleleitungsweg and Goisern. *The path descends on steep (and sometimes slippery) wooden stairs and negotiates the Mühlbach Hölle, a narrow waterfall gorge which cascades down into Hallstatt itself. Cross over a wooden bridge and follow along the cliffside as you descend. The views hereabouts are spectacular.*

The Soleleitungsweg follows the course of the world's oldest long-distance pipeline, an engineering marvel still in use today. The Soleleitung (*sole* meaning brine) was constructed to transport brine the 40 km between Hallstatt and Ebensee where the salt was extracted. It was completed in 1607, prior to which the rock salt had to be transported dangerously on barges and by packhorse. Some of the original 13,000 hollowed out wooden pipes can still be seen in places by the path; the present pipelines of cast-iron or plastic run beneath the path. The waymarked path (#601) forms a small part of the 3,500 km European long-distance alpine hiking trail E4 which runs from Budapest to the Pyrénées.

The level path now winds through woodland high above the Hallstättersee past a disused mine entrance and then under a waterfall and an avalanche shelter. About 5 km from the Rudolfsturm, near Gosaumühle (where there is a bus stop), take a right fork and descend to cross the bridge over the rushing waters of the Gosaubach, some 43 metres below. The route (now waymarked #801) descends gradually and widens, becoming an unsealed road before forking left on a narrow path. Pass a hunting lodge and then descend to meet a minor road. Follow the road left for 50 m and turn right following a 'Soleweg' sign along a farm track. Where this road forks, follow the footpath straight ahead near houses and across pretty meadowland. Turn right along a farm track (signed to Bad Goisern) and at crossroads continue straight on leaving the Soleweg and reaching the river Traun. Follow the river right on the Traunuferweg, passing the new houses of Gorm before turning left to cross the river.

Follow the river right on a gravel path, keeping the railway line on your left. Despite civilization's encroachment, the river and mountain scenery in this area are charming. Turning left onto a paved path, cross the railway and take another gravel path right. Wind between houses and cross a road near a hotel (where lunch could be had) and take a path marked to Hallstätterseeweg. The footpath diverts left steeply uphill (signed 'Ostufer uber Ari-Kogel'). An excellent view of the lake appears before you descend Ari-Kogel and reach a minor road at which you turn left over a bridge crossing the Zlambach. Turn right then left. At another bridge, turn right under the railway and then follow a paved path along the lakeside. The path hugs the lakeside passing Gosaumühle-Obersee station (served by train and, in season, by boat) and becoming a nature trail with botanical information. At one point the lake's banks become so steep that the trail becomes a wooden walkway built over the lake. Cross a suspension bridge with the railway line above, then wind under cliff and railway to reach Hallstatt station. The views of Hallstatt and its mountain backdrop from this last stage of the walk are memorable. Catch the ferry across the lake to return to Hallstatt.

One of the rock formations to be found in the Gletschergarten, on Walk 2.

WALK TWO - THE ECHERNTAL (9 KM; 4.5 HRS)

This relatively short walk leads up the romantic Echerntal and further on to the Salzberg (not to be confused with the city of Salzburg) high valley where an ancient salt mine can be visited. *From Salzbergstrasse in Lahn, take the Malerweg, one of three routes traversing the floor of the Echerntal. You quickly leave civilisation and enter a delightful forest. On your right is a view of the veil falls where the Spraderbach drops a sheer 100 m down the valley wall. Near the Gasthof Dachsteinwarte, leave the forest road and take the Waldmüller-Malerweg, following the Waldbach torrent upstream and soon passing the giant Runenstein (rune stone) on your left. After about 40 minutes of walking, a junction with a sign to Waldbachstrub is reached but, before continuing there, you should detour left on the narrow path which climbs to the Gletschergarten (glacier garden), discovered in 1926.* The garden comprises various rock formations scoured out during the last Ice Age and includes the *Felsentor* (rock door), *Riesenschnecke* (giant snail) and *Riesenkessel* (giant bowl).

A shrine to St Barbara nestles among autumn leaves near the mine entrance.

Return to the track junction and cross the river, taking the steep path to the falls. The Waldbachstrub falls thunder 90 m down the gorge in three stages. After taking in the sight and sound of the falls, return part way down the track to where the famous Gangsteig begins. This is a steep, vertiginous path carved into the valley wall which, despite the 'Danger: experienced hikers only' warnings, can be managed easily by the sure-footed in good weather, assisted by the railings and metal roping provided. The path eventually levels out and meets the forest road (trail #641) where you turn right towards the Salzberg high valley. This traffic-free road commands excellent mountain views with every bend and you are likely to see chamois on the forested slopes.

Continue on the road for several kilometres until reaching the junction with trail #640. The Salzberg salt mine is down valley to the right; up valley are hiking trails to the summit of Plassen (1954 m) and further afield to Gosausee. Take path #640 for about 20 minutes to reach the Knappenhaus, the visitors' entrance to the salt mine. The 1.5 hour guided tour involves donning overalls and sliding down a chute to an illuminated subterranean lake. Opening times vary with the season. *From the salt mine, it is a 10 minute walk down to the Rudolfsturm (see Walk 1) and the funicular landing.* The path passes the famous Hallstatt prehistoric burial grounds with over 2000 graves, of which two are on display. *Now stroll down the serpentine Salzbergweg to Hallstatt, or take the funicular to Lahn.*

WALK THREE - CAVES OF THE DACHSTEIN (15-20 KM; FULL DAY)

In addition to its marvellous scenic attractions, this walk offers a choice of excellent cave excursions, namely the Dachstein Ice Caves, the Mammoth Cave and the Koppenbrüller Cave. Start very early if you propose to see more than one cave and as with Walk 1, bear in mind the time of the last return ferry from Hallstatt station.

The walk begins in Hallstatt Lahn at the pink Kalvarienbergkirche, a Baroque jewel of a church consecrated in 1711. Its beautiful interior contains a crucifixion group from the Guggenbichler School. *The path, waymarked in red and white, leads up into the woods behind the church, sign posted to Schöne Aussicht (beautiful view) where a park bench has been conveniently sited to take in the view of Hallstatt, the lake and the mountains beyond. The path ascends through woods providing filtered lake views. Shortly after passing a small cave and a wooden water trough, the path zigzags uphill (note that it has been rerouted due to an avalanche). Soon you reach the Hirschaualm (840m), an untouched alpine meadow complete with original hut (now only used in summer) and alpine rhododendron. The meadow is surrounded by the massive rock walls of the Zwölferkogel, the Schönbühel and the Rauherkogel. From the hut the way descends on a steep rocky path to meet the Hallstatt/Obertraun road near the Kessel, a karst spring which flows intermittently in a small nature reserve (detour left to view it).*

The rock walls of the Dachstein massif are especially dramatic when lined with snow.

Turn right onto the road and after 25 minutes, as you reach Winkl, look for a path (#615) signed to Krippenstein. Leave the road here but take an unsigned lower branch path which passes behind a barn and skirts farmland then passes behind a federal sports school: look out for grazing deer on the nearby ski slopes. The path disappears briefly but you soon pick up a gravel path through woodland and come to a road which is followed right uphill to the Dachsteinbahn. If visiting the Ice Caves and/ or Mammoth Cave, take the cable- car to the first stage from where both sets of caves are a short walk. The world famous Ice Caves, first explored in 1910, were formed during the Triassic period by the action of water containing carbonic acid on the limestone rock but the spectacular ice shapes were only formed in the last 500 years and the ice is increasing each year. The Mammoth Cave, one of Europe's biggest, has no ice but is atmospherically lit and the tour (in German only) includes a dramatic slide show. A combined ticket may be purchased; arrive early in high season as tickets are limited. Both caves close between mid October and May.

From the Dachsteinbahn lower car park, take the forest trail signposted to Koppenwinkelsee (#3) which follows above the Koppentraun river through dense and romantic woodland, crossing wooden bridges over snow melts. At a junction by the farm buildings of Koppenwinkel-Alm, turn left to reach Koppenwinkelsee, a shallow lake and bird sanctuary which dries up periodically. Continuing on, there are high cliffs to the right of the path and a massive boulder which fell from the cliff face in 1987. Soon after a children's holiday village you reach the Obertraun/Bad Aussee road. Walk towards the river and before the bridge take the path right for a short (20 minutes return) detour to the Koppenbrüllerhöhle. The path gently ascends the deep, narrow gorge of the Koppental to the cave entrance. Underground water roars through the cave (brüllen: to roar) which can be toured by the light of oil lamps. Tours are on the hour until 16. 00 hours; the cave is open from May to September. *Return to the road and cross the Koppentraun river and take the even gravel footpath that veers off slightly to the right of the road. This is the Obertrauner Höhenweg which follows the course of the road and railway high above the valley floor commanding lovely views over Obertraun to the Hallstättersee, Plassen above the Salzberg upper valley, Krippenstein and all the other peaks which enclose the valley.*

If time and energy permit, make the uphill detour (1 hour return) to the Wasserfallwand (waterfall wall) where the valley and mountain views are even more spectacular and, depending on the season, snow melt cascades over a wide wall of rock. Back on the main path, continue until a paved road is reached and turn right, skirting around a graveyard. The path goes through a short tunnel under the railway and then right between the railway and lake, detouring inland and climbing steeply around the private estate of Schloss Grub before emerging at the lakeside. Passing between the imposing face of Sechser-Kogel and the lake, the path soon arrives at the ferry landing for the return trip to Hallstatt.

WALK FOUR - AROUND GOSAUSEE (14 KM; 4. 5 HRS)

This spectacular walk is justifiably one of the Salzkammergut's most famous. With breathtaking views of the Dachstein glacier and the Gosaukamm range reflected in two exquisite lakes, it is a photographer's dream and needs a clear day to do justice to the scenery.

From either of Hallstatt's two bus stops, take Postbus 2572 to Gosaumühle where you change for the connecting 2570 to Gosauschmied. Check the time of the last return buses to Hallstatt. From the Gosauschmied bus stop, cross back over a stream and turn right off the road behind a hotel onto an uphill path signed to Ebenalm (trail #507). The path, waymarked in red-and-white, skirts an artificial lake and climbs a gully through forest before emerging at a road junction

The Gosaukamm rise up dramatically behind Gosau's charming Kirchenwirt.

Evening light adds to the romance of the Hällstatter See.

where the first magnificent views of the dolomitic Gosaukamm range suddenly unfold. Here at the Ebenalm you pass by two huts and take the path which descends to Vorderen Gosausee. Where the path again joins the road, continue left around a hairpin bend and downhill to the lake where you join trail #614 which hugs the lake's northern bank.

At the head of the lake, the path begins its steady climb towards Hinteren Gosausee. You pass the shallow tarn of Gosaulacke on your right and the small Launigg-Wasserfall on your left before the path steepens and then provides glimpses of Hinteren Gosausee at the crest of the summit. Continue to the foot of the lake where seating allows you to contemplate the grandeur of the craggy Dachstein peaks and glaciers mirrored in the lake. The path skirts the lake to the south to reach the hut of See-Alm, which may be open for refreshments depending on the season. From here the return involves retracing your steps and continuing to the foot of Vorderen Gosausee. Alternatively, there is a less direct path (#613) around the other side of Hinteren Gosausee which rejoins the outgoing path at the foot of the lake.

At the foot of Vorderen Gosausee there is a famous viewpoint and a restaurant near the Gosaukamm cable-car station. If time permits you could ride the cable-car up to the Zwieselalm, from where there are panoramic views to the Grossglockner. *Catch the postbus home from either the restaurant or, if necessary, from Gosauschmied a few kilometres down the road.*

NOTES ON THE SALZKAMMERGUT

TYPE OF WALK   Day walks from one base

LENGTH OF WALK   62 kilometres (38.5 miles) over four days

DIFFICULTY   Easy-medium, with occasional steep terrain

BASE   Hallstatt, a lakeside village in northern Austria

PUBLIC TRANSPORT
Train from Salzburg to Hallstatt station; change at Attnang Puchheim on the Salzburg/Linz line. Ferry from Hallstatt station to Hallstatt (ferries meet trains; last ferry about 18.30). Bus from Salzburg to Hallstatt, changing at Bad Ischl and sometimes at Gosaumühle. Postbuses connect Hallstatt to nearby towns of Gosau and Obertraun.

CLIMATE
The Salzkammergut is an alpine region, with heavy snowfalls in winter. July and August can be hot but weather can fluctuate considerably; it is more reliable in early autumn, in September and early October.

MAP
Kompass Wanderkarte 20 *Dachstein: Südliches Salzkammergut* 1:50,000
or Freytag & Berndt Wanderkarte 281 *Dachstein* 1:50,000

PATH
The Soleleitungsweg (which follows the oldest long distance pipeline), waymarked paths, forestry roads.

VILLAGES
Hallstatt (population 1040), Bad Goisern (7500), Obertraun (800).

ACCOMMODATION
There are a choice of small hotels or pensions and plenty of *zimmer frei* (rooms in private houses) in Hallstatt and its surrounds. Hallstatt also has two youth hostels.

CUISINE
Reinanke are caught in the Hallstättersee, while *Forelle* (trout) and *Saibling* come from the rivers nearby. Venison of various types is traditionally served with *Knödeln* (dumplings). Wild garlic known as *Bärlauch* is picked for a short season in spring and appears in a delicious soup (*Bärlauchsuppe*) and in many other dishes. *Topfenbrot* is a local speciality which consists of bread and *Liptauer*, a paprika-flavoured cream cheese. *Most* (Austrian cider) is produced locally.

WILDLIFE
Many bird species including waterbirds, woodpeckers, owls and birds of prey such as golden eagles and bearded vultures. Chamois and alpine ibex can sometimes be seen at high elevation; red deer graze at lower levels. Wildflowers in season.

SPECIAL FEATURES
The Hallstatt Salzbergwerk, the world's oldest operating salt mine; Dachstein Ice Caves; Mammoth Cave; Koppenbrüller Water Cave; waterfalls and Gletschergarten of the Echerntal; the Gosaukamm.

FURTHER READING

WALKING IN THE SALZKAMMERGUT
by Fleur & Colin Speakman, published by Cicerone Press, UK, 1989

DACHSTEIN HIKING GUIDE (ENGLISH TRANSLATION)
by Maximilian Singer, 1995

USEFUL ADDRESSES

TOURISMUSVERBAND HALLSTATT (TOURIST OFFICE)
Postfach 7, A-4830 Hallstatt; Tel: 6134 8208 Fax: 6134 8352

SALZKAMMERGUT ONLINE
http://www.tiscover.com/upperaustria

UMBRIAN HILLTOWNS

A classic walk, rich in history, between Umbria's two most famous hill-towns–Assisi and Spoleto–taking in the idyllic countryside surrounding the Vale of Spoleto and several of Umbria's less visited hilltown treasures.

Landlocked Umbria, 'the green heart of Italy' as it is known, is a rural region featuring quintessential Italian landscapes of cypress trees, vine-yards, undulating farmland, and wooded mountains whose lower slopes are terraced with venerable olive groves. Dotting the landscape are the many hilltowns for which Umbria, like neighbouring Tuscany, has become known to travellers. By comparison with that more celebrated northern region, most of Umbria lies off the well-trod tourist trail and many of its delightful towns remain beguilingly obscure and unvisited.

Much of Umbria's long and sometimes turbulent history has left its mark on the landscape although almost no evidence remains of its 8th century BC settlers, the iron-age Umbrii, a peaceable farming tribe described by Pliny as the oldest in Italy. Their successors, the Etruscans, built hilltowns such as Perugia. Umbria slowly came under Roman sway and in 217 BC the local inhabitants sided with Rome to defeat the Carthaginian Hannibal under the walls of Spoleto. A major road, the Via Flaminia, was built to connect Rome to Rimini on the Adriatic coast. It passed through Umbria, immensely increasing its strategic importance and prosperity through trade; many Roman hilltowns were built on or near this road. In the 6th century, as the Roman Empire crumbled, Umbria became a battleground between Byzantium and the Goths. The defeated Goths were soon replaced by the Lombards who established a Dukedom in Spoleto. During the subsequent dark ages, this region suffered heavily during wars between the Papacy and the Holy Roman Empire. Fortified towns were built on hills for defence, while other settlements clustered around churches or holy sites. Christian-ity flourished early here (St Benedict, the father of monasticism, came from these parts) and Umbria's hills were dotted with sanctuaries and chapels. Assisi became renowned as a place of pilgrimage, prospering when the monk Francis was sanctified in the 13th century.

Our four-day walk begins in Assisi, treading in the footsteps of St Francis, past his mountain hermitage and over Monte Subasio to reach Spello, an exquisite Romanesque hilltown. We then descend to the Vale of Spoleto, a

The limpid beauty of the Fonti di Clitunno, once the summer resort of Roman emperors.

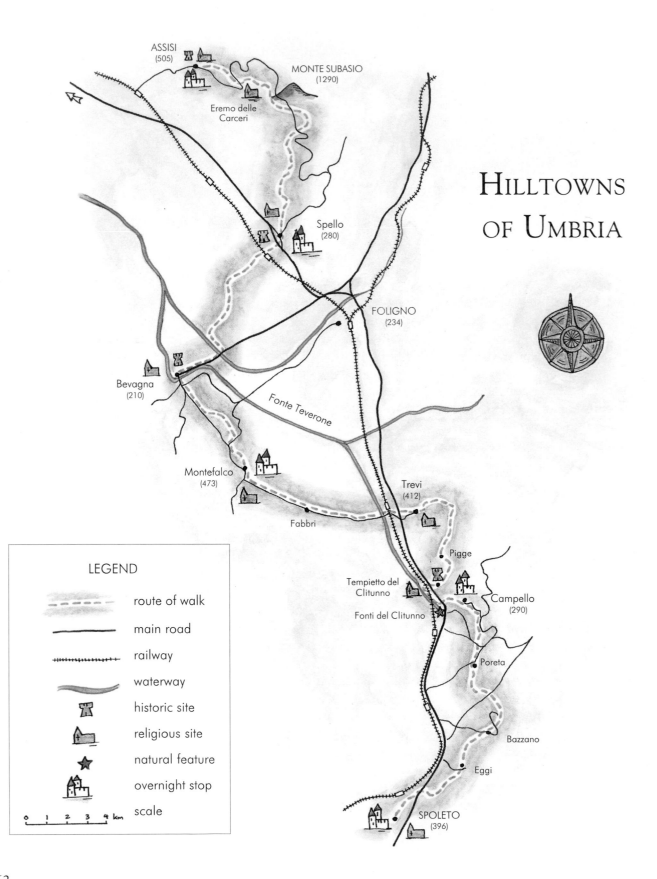

ASSISI
(505)

MONTE SUBASIO
(1290)

Eremo delle
Carceri

Spello
(280)

FOLIGNO
(234)

HILLTOWNS
OF UMBRIA

Bevagna
(210)

Fonte Teverone

Montefalco
(473)

Trevi
(412)

Fabbri

Pigge

Tempietto del
Clitunno

Campello
(290)

Fonti del Clitunno

Poreta

LEGEND

route of walk

main road

railway

waterway

historic site

religious site

natural feature

overnight stop

scale

0   1   2   3   4 km

Bazzano

Eggi

SPOLETO
(396)

beautiful sweep of countryside at the heart of Umbria, and pass through the ancient hilltowns of Bevagna and Montefalco before heading back towards the vale's eastern foothills and Trevi, sited dramatically on the lower reaches of Monte Pettino. Between Trevi and Spoleto, our route follows the *Sentiero degli Ulivi*, 'the olive path', up and down terraced hillsides, through ancient hamlets and past forsaken monasteries and castles. Walkers should not expect true remoteness here: civilisation, however rustic, will usually be within sight. One of the many pleasures afforded by this journey is the engaging friendliness of the Umbrian people, as yet untested by the strains of excess tourism. Another is the taste of the traditional Umbrian cuisine which is simple and closely wedded to the immediate landscape. You may well encounter individuals harvesting wild asparagus or searching the forest undergrowth for black truffles.

A few words need to be said about route-finding, though it would be difficult to become dangerously lost on this walk. The first day's walk over Monte Subasio is well waymarked with the familiar red-and-white horizontal stripes. Between Spello and Trevi, the unwaymarked route follows country roads and lanes. Between Trevi and Spoleto, another officially waymarked walking route is followed, however the waymarking is sporadic and at all times the use of an appropriate map is strongly advised.

DAY ONE - ASSISI TO SPELLO (14 KM; 7 HRS)

Our route begins in Assisi which deserves a full exploration with at least one night spent there. Detailed information on its treasures can be gained from a myriad of guide books, for Assisi is one of Italy's most visited places. Or rather it was before the September 1997 earthquake damaged many of its buildings, some of which have been closed for repair.

Assisi, sitting enticingly atop a foothill of Monte Subasio, was already ancient during St Francis' lifetime (1182-1226). Occupied by the Umbrii and then the Etruscans, it became the Roman city of Assisium. A glimpse of this is seen in the 1st century BC facade of the Tempio di Minerva (now a church), one of the most perfect Roman facades in Italy. It is the Basilica of San Francesco, however, that the pilgrims come to visit. Composed of two churches built one above the other between 1228 and 1253, it is an astounding medieval architectural feat sited on the western fringe of Assisi and it dominates distant views of the city. Beneath the basilica lies the crypt in which St Francis was buried. The two churches were frescoed by Italy's greatest 13th and 14th century painters: Cimabue, Giotto, Martini and the Lorinzettis. Other sites to visit include the Rocca Maggiore (the medieval fort that crowns the city), the austere and heavily buttressed Gothic church of Santa Chiara (founder of the Order of the Poor Clares) and the Duomo San Rufino with its fine Romanesque campanile and facade.

Today's walk, mostly on mountain and forest paths, is entirely within the Parco Regionale del Subasio and involves over 800 metres of ascent. Lunch supplies should be purchased before setting out; there are no shops en route. *The route leaves from the Porta Cappuccini on the Via Eremo delle*

The Tempio di Minerva stands as a reminder of Assisi's Roman past.

The path leaving Assisi offers a good view back to the Rocca Maggiore.

Carceri to the city's east. Outside the gate you immediately turn sharp left onto a red-and-white waymarked track (#50) which initially follows the city wall up to the Rocca Minore. Ignore a left diversion (#51) and ascend steeply up a stony track for almost an hour with great views of the Vale of Spoleto to the right. The path levels and presently meets the Assisi/Monte Subasio road. Turn right and follow this downhill, and soon detour slightly to reach the Eremo dei Carceri. Set in a thickly wooded gully, the hermitage, with its minute church hollowed out of the rock, became an occasional retreat for Francis and his followers. Since the 14th century the Eremo has been a 'working' monastery and the monks still live off the alms they receive, but Francis's tiny cell (carcere means 'enclosed space') has been preserved along with his stone bed and wooden pillow.

Back at the road, turn right and follow it uphill for five minutes then, at a sharp bend, turn left uphill on a woodland path. Later the path swings right and eventually meets a track and reaches the Rifugio di Vallonica (1059 m). You soon pass some old foundations and a water trough. The path now becomes less distinct over treeless terrain; veer left over a saddle, following waymarks on poles. (A brief diversion is recommended: head towards a promontory marked by a cross for superb views back to Assisi.) Head uphill towards communications towers to rejoin the road; follow this right briefly then veer left onto trail #50. To the south are marvellous views of the distant Sibillines, part of the Apennine range which forms the backbone of Italy. Presently the path skirts to the left of

Spello overflows with beautifully preserved Romanesque buildings and streetscapes.

crater and then swings right to meet up with another trail and regain the road. Cross the road, look for the path (which can be hard to find) and descend to reach the Fuente Bregno at the 1000 m contour line where there are good views, a water hut and a picnic table. Continue SE downhill and zigzag down to cross the gully and then contour the hill. The waymarking improves now as you descend through low scrub and there are superb views of Spello, the Vale of Spoleto and the distant Martani Hills. The way becomes a broad stony path through olive groves and, shortly before reaching Spello, a paved road.

The stretched triangular form of Spello, protected by its much rebuilt walls, appears to rise gently out of the surrounding countryside, graceful rather than imposing. It has a Roman pedigree as Hispellium, built in the 1st century BC, but Spello is nonetheless an exquisite Romanesque hilltown. Now a quiet backwater, its six 12th and 13th century churches underline its former importance. While the entire town repays careful exploration, the undoubted highlight is the Cappella Baglioni in the church of Santa Maria Maggiore frescoed in 1501 by Pinturicchio. Restored in 1978, the fresco sequence of Jesus' birth glows with colourful detail.

DAY TWO - SPELLO TO MONTEFALCO (18 KM; 5 HRS)

Today's walk in the Vale of Spoleto is unwaymarked but confines itself to minor roads and farm lanes. The day's main objectives are the beautiful hilltowns of Bevagna (a suitable lunch stop) and Montefalco, with its commanding views of the surrounding countryside. *Leave Spello on the Via Consolare and through the Porta Consolare over which are three statues, originally from a Roman tomb. Outside Spello's walls, head towards the train station on the Via Ca' Rapillo. The road crosses the Via Centrale Umbra, goes under the autostrada and over the railway line just north of Spello station. It becomes the Via Acquatino which is followed through Spello's outskirts and farmland for 2.5 km when you should turn left at a crossroads onto the Via Cascina Piermarini. At an intersection keep straight on the Via Lago di Fiastre, walk straight through the hamlet of Budino and take a lesser road straight on where the main road curves left. In 450 m you reach the embankment of the Fosse Topino; turn left and follow the fosse (canal) for just over 1 km until you meet the busy Foligno-Bevagna road. Climb up the embankment and cross the bridge. From here Bevagna is almost 2.5 km straight ahead and is entered through the Porta di Foligno.*

Even smaller and far less known than Spello, Bevagna is rich in heritage and should be explored at leisure. Traces of its Roman origins as a way station on the Via Flaminia are never far from the surface. Fragments of a Roman theatre are to be found in a curved row of houses lining the Vicolo dell'Anfiteatro. Nearby are the remains of a temple and in Via Porta Guelfa can be found Roman baths with a stunning mosaic floor featuring lobsters, dolphins and other sea creatures. Bevagna's beautiful medieval Piazza Silvestri separates two fine Romanesque churches, San Michele and San Silvestro, both built in austere style by Binello in the late 12th century. Also fronting the piazza is the Gothic Palazzo dei Consoli, its interior converted to a theatre said to be the most beautiful auditorium in Umbria.

The doorway to San Michele, one of Bevagna's two fine 12th century churches.

Leave Bevagna through the Porta Todi and take the road towards Bastardo which crosses a small bridge. At a junction almost 1 km on, continue straight ahead on the more minor road to Montefalco. Take the second gravel lane to the left which winds traffic-free through idyllic countryside and affords lovely views of cypress-lined slopes. After 1.5 km at a T-junction, turn left uphill then first right onto a paved road. Turn right at the next junction and ascend to the hamlet of Monte Pennino, where the road from Bevagna is rejoined and followed uphill. After this hamlet, look for a track veering slightly left downhill. This is a pleasant short cut which reaches Montefalco's walls near the Porta San Agostino.

Montefalco (or *Falcon's Mount*) is known locally as 'the balcony of Umbria' and it lives up to its names, affording panoramic 360° views. Climb to the top of the Torre Comunale, on the Piazza del Comune, to best take in the vista. The piazza is unusual for its irregular shape and occupies the very crown of the hill. Montefalco's heyday was in the 14th century when it became a refuge to Spoleto's papal governors following the popes' move to Avignon. The 14th century former church of San Francisco and its attached museum are Montefalco's star attractions. The church is frescoed with scenes from the life of St Francis by the 15th century Florentine artist, Benozzo Gozzoli. These frescos borrow from Giotto's cycle in Assisi, but are nevertheless considered to be among the great Renaissance fresco cycles for their radiance and controlled narrative.

Montefalco, known for the robust red wines produced nearby.

DAY THREE - MONTEFALCO TO CAMPELLO (21 KM; 7 HRS)

Today's journey again involves road walking across the Vale of Spoleto to Trevi, where lunch may be purchased. From Trevi, the waymarked route ascends and descends through tiny hamlets and crumbling ruins on the vale's fringe before reaching Campello. *Head out of Montefalco through the Porta Frederico II, turn right along the Via Frederico II to reach Via Cavior and take the second road to the left, the Via Giuseppe Verdi.* On the corner is the church of Santa Chiara, one of eight saints born in Montefalco (her mummified body is in a clear casket above the altar). *Walk down Via Verdi past the tiny Sant'Illuminata which contains frescos by Francesco Melanzio, a local 16th century artist. Pass through the Porta San Leonardo to the Viale Marconi which soon merges with a larger road. Continue on and then turn left at Via Evangelista Correcelli, presently passing the Monastero di San Fortunato, a Franciscan convent set among holly trees.* The 15th century church is decorated with frescos by Gozzoli and Tiberio d'Assisi and is worth a diversion.

Ignoring a left turn to Turri, continue on the minor road signposted to Fabbri. The small vineyards you walk past on the Fabbri road are part of the tiny area which produces the renowned red wine, Sagrantino. You pass through Fabbri with its 16th century *rocca* (fort) and *torre* (tower) on your right. The rocca has been restored by the Azienda Vinicola which has also constructed a large modern cellar under the piazza where local wines may be tasted. *Continue towards Trevi crossing numerous fosse.* Trevi soon appears in the distance, with its ancient houses seeming to cascade down the hillside on which they are perched. *Where the main road sweeps off and over the railway line, take a minor road straight on to reach a foot passage underneath the railway. From the train station you can catch a bus which wends 4 km uphill to the heart of Trevi. Alternatively, walk through Borgo Trevi, the suburb around the station, cross the Via Flaminia and begin the uphill walk towards Trevi's lowest entry, the Porta di San Fabiano. Once inside Trevi's outer medieval wall, it is all uphill as you negotiate a maze of patterned cobblestone lanes.*

Trevi may or may not be the Roman town Trebiae. Under the Roman emperor Diocletian, Christianity was promoted here by an Armenian priest Sant'Emiliano, Trevi's patron saint who was martyred by being drowned in the nearby Fonte di Clitunno. The 12th century church of Sant'Emiliano occupies the high point of Trevi. The lanes radiating from the church are particularly atmospheric and close; the nearby Piazza Mazzini, Trevi's handsome and spacious centre, provides an attractive contrast.

The town of Trevi, perched on a steep hillside among venerable olive groves.

Leave this piazza by the Via Roma and, from the piazza outside Trevi's walls, follow the Via Coste San Paolo then fork left up towards the Impantivi Sportivi. Proceed straight uphill through olive groves on a track waymarked #60 Costa S. Paulo. Keep looking back for the changing views of Trevi as you climb. When you reach a fork, take the right path and turn right at a junction just below Costa San Paulo. We now follow the Sentiero degli Ulivi, marked S.U. in red on the map. Take a minor path to the right through woodland to join a wider track downhill to a clearing with a water trough. Continue downhill to reach the isolated Romanesque church of Sant'Arcangelo. Proceed down between church and house on a narrow footpath. At a hairpin bend join a wider track and then turn left on a minor road down to a junction. Take the leftmost track uphill and at a Y-junction go right downhill, passing below a cemetery and La Cura church. Head downhill through Pigge and, keeping the village church on your right, regain the track at the corner of a communal washhouse. This joins a minor road which eventually becomes a grass track and reaches Pissignano. It is worth an uphill detour to wander through the narrow streets within the 13th century castle, partly ruined but containing many residences now restored and occupied as an artist colony. *From Pissignano take the road down to the highway; cross it and turn right onto a parallel road to soon reach the beautiful Tempietto di Clitunno.*

This tiny church, which makes use of recycled Roman columns and was long thought to be Roman, possibly dates from the 5th century and contains faded remnants of Byzantine frescos from the 8th century, possibly Umbria's oldest. *Follow the Via Flaminia south for 1 km or so to reach the Fonti di Clitunno.* Natural underground springs collect here to form the source of the river Clitumnus. The Romans plunged animals in the Fonti for purification prior to sacrifice and Emperors Caligula and Claudius built villas and temples here of which nothing remains. Much later, the poet Byron and the artist Corot found inspiration in the waters here. Despite the proximity of the highway, the souvenirs and the occasional tourist coach, the springs and the willow-lined lake retain a romantic charm. Overnight hotel accommodation can be found to the south of the Fonti in Sette Camini near the Campello sul Clitunno railway station. Alternatively take the road uphill to reach the several hamlets comprising Campello sul Clitunno where accommodation can also be found.

DAY FOUR - CAMPELLO TO SPOLETO (20 KM; 6.5 HRS)

Today's route returns to, and follows, the sporadically waymarked Sentiero degli Ulivi all the way to Spoleto. There are no large villages en route so you should buy lunch provisions before setting out. *From your hotel, find your way to Via Dante Alighieri in the Villa/Ravale area of Campello. Wind uphill past lovely old villas and at a hairpin bend take a narrow path straight uphill through dense woodland for 15 minutes. Turn left on reaching a grassy path and, where this emerges at a lane, turn right towards Campello Alto. The route skirts left of this fortified castle and village but the short detour should be made for the panoramic views of the patchwork fields below.*

Return to the road and at a major intersection take the right-hand road to Lenano whose church of San Lorenzo contains 15th century frescoes. Past the village, take a path right and descend through olive groves. The waymarking seems to be absent hereabouts; the objective is to reach the village of Poreta by exiting the olive groves onto the Bianca/Silvignano road near the branch road to Poreta. Take this branch road through Poreta, which is dominated by its 14th century castle. Ignore a road left to La Piaggia and take a footpath left at a shrine. Ignore a path branching left after 300 m (waymarked #11); continue until you have passed the end of the wooded spur and entered olive groves. Turn left (E) to contour the base of the spur and then right (S) after 600 m. Cross the paved road near the church of Santa Maria di Reggiano, built upon Roman ruins

Campello Alto, high above the Vale of Spoleto, still has its fortified walls intact.

and containing 15th century frescoes.

Pass the church and continue straight uphill at a crossroads. Fork right and continue to Bazzano Superiore, where you keep the church on your left and take the paved road right. At the next hamlet take the lower path right and pass the Romanesque church of Santa Maria, the path winding down between houses. Take a footpath leading off from a communal washhouse, cross an unpaved road and continue downhill. At a multi-path junction, continue down right and through the village of Bazzano Inferiore, overlooked by its 14th century castle. The village has a grocery shop and a bus service to Eggi and Spoleto. Turn left past the church and, at the end of the village, go left uphill at a fork and continue through woods. At an olive grove, take a track left and wind down to Eggi with its 14-15th century hill castle.

From Eggi, make your way down to the Eggi quarry which is visible from a distance. Poorly waymarked, this could involve some trial and error. Cross the entrance to the unfortunately ugly quarryworks and climb the track up the other side of the gully to a clearing beneath the scarred rockface. Follow a track off to the right and very soon take a narrow footpath on the left which climbs steeply through dense forest (there is a fixed rope to aid the ascent). The path comes out at the disused Spoleto to Norcia railway line, a scenic mountain line which was closed in the 1960s. Now a footpath, the line can be followed (through two short tunnels and over viaducts) 3 km to the outskirts of Spoleto, affording some excellent views of the surrounding forest and farmland along the way. The line ends near the motorway; from here, follow signs to the town or to the station.

With spring comes the painstaking task of pruning each olive tree.

Spoleto is best known as the host to Italy's most famous arts festival, the Festival dei Due Mondi. The Roman colony of Spoletium was founded in 241 BC on the Via Flaminia. Its Roman grandeur is evidenced by its well-preserved walls, a restored Roman theatre, the Arco di Druso (an arch built in honour of emperor Tiberius' son, Drusus), the remains of an amphitheatre and, now covered by the Piazza Garibaldi, a Roman bridge of Travertine marble. Spoleto prospered from the 6th to 8th centuries as the seat of a Lombard dukedom which eventually dominated much of central Italy. Annihilated by Barbarossa in 1155, Spoleto came under papal authority a century later and generally remained so until the Papal States were absorbed into the kingdom of Italy in 1860.

Spoleto is an exquisite Romanesque city and, as with Assisi, a guidebook is essential. Even the lower town, bombed during WW2, has much to offer the visitor including the 4th century Basilica of San Salvatore, one of Italy's first Christian churches which was modified in the 9th century reusing many Roman materials. Just inside the town's walls, the 12th century church of San Gregorio Maggiore is dedicated to Bishop Gregory, one of the many Christians martyred in the nearby amphitheatre.

In the upper town, within the courtyard of the Archbishops' Palace, Sant'Eufemia is possibly Umbria's best preserved Romanesque church. Its unadorned interior belies its complex design and it is the only Umbrian church with a *matroneum*, a gallery designed to segregate the women. The interior of the 12th century Duomo, on the other hand, is a lavish Baroque affair rebuilt in the 17th century. It contains frescos by Pinturicchio and by Fra Filippo Lippi, the latter being buried in the cathedral. Of Spoleto's other noteworthy buildings, make sure you see the remarkable Ponte delle Torri, a ten-span medieval bridge built over a Roman aqueduct, best viewed from the rocca above the town.

Notes on Umbrian Hilltowns

TYPE OF WALK	One way
LENGTH OF WALK	73 kilometres (45 miles); four days
DIFFICULTY	A medium grade walk, with several steep ascents
START	Assisi, the home of St Francis
FINISH	Spoleto, a beautiful Romanesque city

PUBLIC TRANSPORT
Assisi and Spoleto both have railway stations; change at Foligno to connect. The town of Assisi is a 2-km bus trip or walk from the station.

LUGGAGE   Leave excess luggage at Assisi station.

CLIMATE
The climate here is temperate and so the walking season is a long one, although it could be unpleasantly hot at the height of summer. Spring and autumn are ideal for walking.

MAPS
Kompass No. 663 *Perugia Deruta* 1:50,000 and IGM 131 I SO *Trevi*, II NO *Campello*, & II SO *Spoleto*

PATH
Waymarked footpaths, gravel tracks, minor roads, a section of disused railway. The sections of road could be travelled by taxi or public transport.

SHORTER VARIANT (see Days 1 & 4)
A two-day version: *Train and bus to Assisi*; 1 - walk over Monte Subasio to Spello; 2 - *train to Campello sul Clitunno*; walk the *Sentiero degli Ulivi* from Campello to Spoleto.

VILLAGES
Assisi (population 25,500), **Spello** (8,000), Bevagna (4,750), **Montefalco** (4,900), Trevi (7,650), Pissignano, **Campello** (2,300), Poreta, **Spoleto** (38,000).

ACCOMMODATION
There are hotels and pensiones at the suggested overnight stops. Limited accommodation is also available at Bevagna and Trevi. Accommodation is extremely scarce in Assisi at Easter and during

the 3-4 October Feast of St Francis, and also in Spoleto during the two-week Due Mondi festival in June/July.

CUISINE
Local wild mushrooms and black truffles (*tartufo nero*) are often used in pasta dishes, in *frittata* (omelette) or on *crostini* (toasted bread). Pork and wild boar (*cinghiale*) often appear on the menu. Trevi and Spoleto produce excellent olive oil, considered among Italy's finest. Umbrian wines are produced in small quantities and so are not well known abroad; the exception is the wonderful dry red Sagrantino which is produced from the slopes of Montefalco.

WILDLIFE
Not much wildlife remains after centuries of hunting; there are some squirrels, foxes and wild boar. Orchids and fritillaries bloom on Monte Subasio in May/June, while poppies, violets, cyclamen and other flowers abound in the Vale of Spoleto. Trees include holly, oak, cypress and Aleppo pine.

SPECIAL FEATURES
Basilica di San Francesco and Rocca Maggiore in Assisi; Eremo delle Carceri (St Francis's hermitage); Pinturicchio frescos in Spello; Roman mosaic in Bevagna; Museo Civico in Montefalco; the ancient Tempietto and Fonti del Clitunno near Campello; Spoleto's Sant'Eufemia and Duomo, and the Ponti delle Torri nearby.

FURTHER READING

UMBRIA
by Jonathan Keates, published by George Philip, 1991.

WALKING AND EATING IN TUSCANY AND UMBRIA
by James Lasdun & Pia Davies, published by Penguin, 1997.

A PIEDI IN UMBRIA
by Stefano Ardito, published by Edizione Iter (in Italian).

USEFUL ADDRESSES

CAI (CLUB ALPINO ITALIANO)
Perugia office - via della Gabbia, 9 Tel/fax: 075) 5730334
Foligno office - via Piermarini, 3
Spoleto office - vicolo Pianciani, 4 Tel/fax: 0743) 220433

ASSOCIAZIONE SENTIERO ITALIA
via San Gervasio 12, I-50131 Firenze FI

AZIENDA DI PROMOZIONE TURISTICA (TOURIST OFFICE)
Piazza del Comune, Assisi; Tel: 075) 812450 Fax: 075) 813727

THE DOLOMITES

A selection of superb high-level walks amid the stupendous mountains, blue glacial lakes and fertile valley scenery surrounding Cortina d'Ampezzo, Italy's foremost mountain resort.

The Dolomites are the most beautiful mountains in Italy, indeed it has been said, the world. Named after French geologist Deodat de Dolomieu, who described their mineral composition in 1788, these peaks were once coral and marine sediments deposited during the Triassic period (250-200 million years ago) in what was then a tropical sea separating Europe from Africa. Much later the Dolomite rocks (along with the Alps) were deformed and uplifted by continental collision; glaciation and erosion did the rest. The Dolomites have a distinctive verticality: tall sharp-edged towers and spires of rock rise abruptly from gentle alpine pastureland or from rocky tundra plateaux. The mountains change colour in the sunlight and glow pink and purple in brilliant sunsets, a sight known as the 'alpenglow'.

Cortina d'Ampezzo is the capital of the northeastern Dolomites. Having gained prestige after hosting the 1956 Winter Olympics, Cortina is now Italy's most fashionable winter resort, a fact attested to by the elegance of its shops and visitors, best observed during the evening *passeggiata*. Cortina is set in the sunny basin of the Valle d'Ampezzo on the river Boite, encircled by dramatic mountains towering nearly 2000 m above the town. The three pyramidal peaks of the Tofane group rise up from the west: Tofana di Rozes, Tofana di Mezzo and Tofana di Dentro. To the north is the red blockish bulk of the Croda Rossa. Cristallo dominates the northeast, massive Sorapiss the east and the more shapely Anteleo the southeast. To the south and south west the mountains are lower but no less compelling, particularly the Cinque Torri whose stone towers resemble an archeological ruin from a distance.

You may notice bilingual (Italian and German) and sometimes trilingual (Ladin) signage in this former border area. Ladin is an ancient Romansch or Raeto-Roman tongue, derived from the integration of the Latin of the Roman conquerors with the language of the earlier Celtic inhabitants whom the Romans called Raetians. It is still spoken in some of the Dolomites' more isolated valleys including the Valle di Fanes (visited on Walk 5). The Ladin culture is rich in poetry and mythology passed

The Dolomites feature a superb network of walking paths with many awe-inspiring views.

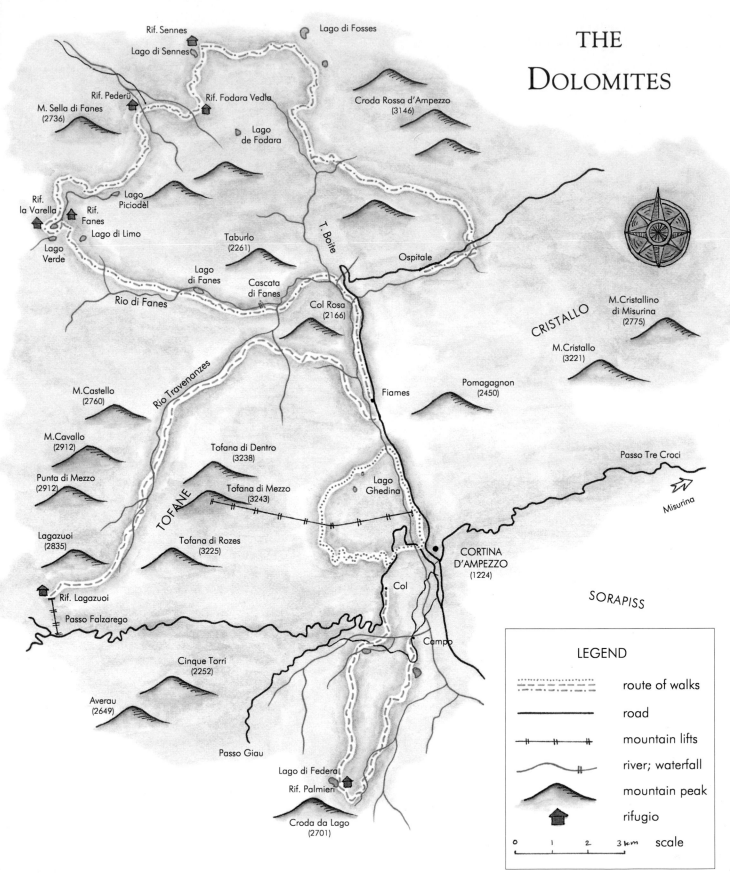

THE

DOLOMITES

Rif. Sennes

Lago di Fosses

Lago di Sennes

Rif. Pederü

Rif. Fodara Vedla

M. Sella di Fanes
(2736)

Croda Rossa d'Ampezzo
(3146)

Lago
de Fodara

Rif.
la Varella

Lago
Piciodèl

Rif.
Fanes

Lago di Limo

Taburlo
(2261)

T. Boite

Lago
Verde

Lago
di Fanes

Cascata
di Fanes

Ospitale

CRISTALLO

M.Cristallino
di Misurina
(2775)

Rio di Fanes

Col Rosa
(2166)

M. Cristallo
(3221)

Rio Travenanzes

M.Castello
(2760)

Fiames

Pomagagnon
(2450)

M.Cavallo
(2912)

Tofana di Dentro
(3238)

Passo Tre Croci

Punta di Mezzo
(2912)

TOFANE

Tofana di Mezzo
(3243)

Lago
Ghedina

Misurina

Lagazuoi
(2835)

Tofana di Rozes
(3225)

Rif. Lagazuoi

Col

Passo Falzarego

CORTINA
D'AMPEZZO
(1224)

SORAPISS

Campo

Cinque Torri
(2252)

Averau
(2649)

Passo Giau

Lago di Federa

LEGEND

Rif. Palmieri

.... route of walks

Croda da Lago
(2701)

──────── road

─⌗──⌗──⌗─ mountain lifts

river; waterfall

mountain peak

rifugio

0   1   2   3 km   scale

down orally through the centuries. *Regole*, an ancient system of communal land management also dates back to Celtic times and is still practised around Cortina today. Lands administered by the Regole cannot be subdivided or reassigned, so protecting grazing and forestry rights.

Once part of the Republic of Venice, Cortina joined the Hapsburg Tyrol in 1511 and generally remained within the Austro-Hungarian Empire until WW1 when battle was waged on the very mountains. Walks 3 and 4 provide grim reminders–barbed wire, trenches, tunnels, galleries and rusty cans–of the fierce war of attrition waged between Austria and Italy in the most bitter mountain weather conditions. At the war's end the Austrian Dolomites were ceded to Italy. The region's architecture, language and cuisine continue to bespeak its Tyrolean heritage making for a fascinating experience for the visitor.

With an exceptional infrastructure of paths, *rifugios* (basic mountain hotels), public and mountain transport as well as many tourist facilities, the Ampezzo Dolomites provide unlimited walking opportunities. The walks selected require no special expertise or equipment providing they are not attempted when snow lies on the path. Of course, the usual precautions for walking in mountain terrain apply. May the weather be kind to you!

Walk One - Lago Ghedina (11.5 km; 4 hrs)

This easy half-day circular walk leads you beneath Tofane's eastern flanks to picturesque Lago Ghedina, nestled in a beautiful forest setting, before you descend to a dramatic crossing of the Torrente Boite.

From Cortina's 1775 parish church, descend to the river and cross at the nearby bridge. Cross the road and follow a lane up between houses, then cross another road and continue uphill. Turn left on a lane just past the first buildings and, at the bend, cross 100 m of meadow and turn left onto the road. Soon turn right at a sign to Lago Ghedina (Path #407); this road winds uphill with lovely views of Cortina and beyond. An hour or so from the start, you pass the base of a chairlift. Path #406 joins in at the left and the Tofane range looms ahead.

At the end of the bitumen, pass a signpost and keep right on #410, now a gravel track into the Val Druscie. You soon pass a water spout and descend gently. Head straight through a path junction, with a wonderful view of needle formations up to the left. At Ra Forzèla (1670 m), take the narrow path #410 right, descending through woodland scattered with alpenrose. Continue downhill until a signpost directs you right to Lago Ghedina, where you turn right onto the road. Left of the lakeside restaurant (open seasonally), steps lead down to a path around the lake, from where the view of the lake, with Tofane in the distance, is prettiest.

From the parking area, cross the paved road and pick up path #416/410 signed to La Vera. 150 m downhill, turn left onto the grassy path #416. Turn right onto a vehicular track and then left onto a footpath (still on #416). This descends to the Torrente Boite, crossed by a wooden bridge, a delightful spot for a picnic. Climb the opposite bank to soon meet the main road and turn right. At

Autumn foliage brings out the green hue of Lago Ghedina.

Early snow dusts the scree above Lago di Federa.

Spring gentians are picked to make a local liqueur.

a nearby parking bay take the side road uphill, then immediately turn right onto path #208, a pleasant level footpath/cycleway which follows the old train route back to the centre of Cortina.

WALK TWO - LAGO DI FEDERA (13.25 KM; 4.5 HRS)

This is a fairly easy circular walk beneath the Croda da Lago south of Cortina whose high point (in both senses) is the delightful Lago di Federa. In summer, the Rifugio Palmieri, nestled on the lake's eastern shore, allows for a lunch or overnight stop.

Take Bus 3 from Cortina to Col. Backtrack to the Falzarego road, walk south uphill for 1.25 km and take path #451 left. After 300 m turn right onto a track (#428) and after crossing the Rio Costeana on the Ponte Alto, leave the track right for an unnumbered path which soon joins track #430. Continue ahead until a crossroads where you should detour left a short distance to reach tiny Lago d'Aial where refreshments can be bought at the Bar Lago d'Aial. Return to the crossroads and turn left onto #431, a car-free road which soon becomes a footpath. Follow # 431 south all the way to the Lago di Federa, a constant ascent through woodland. About half way it ascends steeply left of the rock outcrops, the Becco d'Aial (a short detour right) and over the Alpe di Formin. The path quality improves over the last 1.5 km to the lake, reached in 2 hours or so. Pristine Lago di Federa (2046 m) is terraced above the Cortina basin and below the sheer and imposing rocky spine of the Croda da Lago. There is a path around the lake, fringed with larch and pine, from where there are superb views north to the giant peaks of Cristallo, Sorapiss and Antelao on the other side of the Valle d'Ampezzo. Save some film for the return journey which leaves the lake near the rifugio.

The return path 432 is a car-free forestry track which descends the Val Federa to Campo on Cortina's outskirts, a walk of around 2 hours. You first emerge from forest at Malga Federa, a summer farm (fresh water from tap) with wonderful views over the Cortina area and behind to the Croda da Lago. Back into forest, the descent continues and the Torrente Federa is crossed near cascades. Ignoring the many side trails and logging tracks you will reach the junction of paths 432 and 428 which could be followed to return to Col where you commenced. Otherwise continue on #432 down to Campo di Sotto. You may wish to detour right a short distance (signposted) to see the lovely Lago di Pianoze where there is a chalet. Local bus #2 returns to Cortina from Campo or you could walk back along path #208 which parallels the Torrente Boite and the main road.

WALK THREE - TRE CIME DI LAVAREDO (14 KM; 6.5 HRS)

This moderate grade, high-level circular walk around the extraordinary Tre Cime di Lavaredo and the Monte Paterno is considered to be one of the Dolomites' classics and is deservedly popular. The walk commences at Rifugio Auronzo, reached from Cortina by a seasonal bus trip with a change at Misurina (operates from July to mid-September). Check return times before setting out or book a rifugio bed!

The peaks of Tre Cime di Lavaredo dominate the postcard view from Rifugio Locatelli.

From Rifugio Auronzo (2320 m), it is a level 2 km walk along a traffic-free track (path #101/104) to Rifugio Lavaredo (2344 m) situated beneath the Croda Passaporto. You walk under the four (not three!) towering spires of Tre Cime which dominate this furrowed limestone terrain; to the south are admirable views of the Cadini group of spires and needles. *Ten minutes after the rifugio, veer right to head SE along the less walked #104 passing left of a tiny lake. This WW1 muletrack descends into the pasture of the Pian di Lavaredo and, after meeting path #107, climbs to reach Lago di Cengia and a monument. Take path #104 N to cross a barren slope and zigzag steeply up to numerous WW1 fortifications. Continue climbing to reach the Forcella Pian di Cengia (2522 m) at a path junction.* Detour right for Rifugio Pian di Cengia, taking in the exceptional panorama en route and noting Monte Popera's tiny glacier visible due E. You traverse a rock ledge on wooden planks before contouring left to reach the charming rifugio where simple meals are available.

Return to the Forcella Pian di Cengia where there are wonderful views NW to the Tre Scarperi group. Now follow #101 NW, descending a steep gully and then crossing the scree of Monte Paterno's northern flanks. You pass above a tiny vivid blue glacial tarn and after a short climb you encounter two more such tarns, the Laghi dei Piani. A gentle climb takes you to the popular Rifugio Locatelli under the Torre Toblin. Occupying a strategic position near the battle front, the original building was burnt during WW1 hostilities. The views of the Croda Rossa (W), the Cristallo group (SW) and, of course, the Tre Cime di Lavaredo are exceptional and you will want to linger for a while.

The return to Rifugio Auronzo on path #105 (Alta Via #4) around Tre Cime's western flanks takes longer than the more direct #101 but is less crowded. You descend into a flat rocky cirque, cross a stream and ascend again, crossing barren rock and traversing scree before reaching the Forcella Col di Mezzo (2315 m) where the views are panoramic. The path now tends SE and provides distant views of the Sorapiss, Antelao and Marmarole peaks en route back to the rifugio.

WALK FOUR - VAL TRAVENANZES (16.5 KM; 7 HRS)

Make use of a cable car to gain initial height for the spectacular descent of the Val Travenanzes, beneath the towering walls of the Tofane group. With its stunning scenery and wildlife, this route deserves to be better known. Take plenty of food for you are some distance from civilisation. The route commences at the Passo Falzarego, 13 km from Cortina (a bus service operates from July) and finishes near Fiames where you can return to Cortina on a local bus. Passo Falzarego (2105 m) lies beneath the Lagazuoi Piccolo, one of the main theatres of WW1 combat in the Dolomites. From the pass, looking north to the Lagazuoi Piccolo, you can see two rock slides caused by Austrian and Italian mine explosions. Take the Lagazuoi cable car to the summit of Lagazuoi Piccolo (2752 m) to be met with one of the Dolo-

The lunar landscape of Val Travenanzes, once the backdrop for WW1 battles.

mites' most stunning panoramas: NE to the Tofane, E to Sorapiss and SE to the Croda da Lago, Cinque Torri, Nuvolau and Averau.

From the Rifugio Lagazuoi, take path #401 zigzagging down over scree and late snow below the rifugio and turn right at the path junction. You pass through a WW1 battle zone beside cutaway galleries and beneath tunnel openings in the mountain walls, with the Monte Lagazuoi Grande ahead. *Continue on #401 at a path junction at the Forcella Lagazuoi (2573 m) to soon reach the Forcella Travenanzes (2507 m).* Chamois can often be spotted hereabouts. *Continue ENE on #401/402. At a junction you fork left on #401 with the awesome pyramid of the Tofana di Rozes ahead to begin a gradual descent of the U-shaped glacial Val Travenanzes.* This landscape, seemingly barren, is home to tiny alpine rock flowers and, further on, the light woodland shelters alpenrose. *You pass the ruins of an earlier rifugio and a junction for the Scala del Menighel where you keep left. Soon after path #17 joins left from Monte Cavallo, you reach the abandoned shepherd's hut (now an emergency shelter) at Ex Malga Travenanzes.* Look and listen out for the resident marmot colony hereabouts.

The route follows the course of the Rio Travenanzes and then crosses it (you may need to remove boots for this). To your right (E) is the flank of Tofana di Mezzo, to the west is Monte Cavallo with water cascading off the rock walls after rain or snow. *The valley sides close and steepen as you descend and you cross sides of the torrent twice more before the path curves E and steepens.* Ahead is the Croda Rossa. Shortly after you enter woodland, an unsigned detour left down to a footbridge over the Rio Travenanzes offers dramatic chasm views; alternatively, you might detour further along to the Ponte de Cadoris for a similar view. *At a junction take path #408 right to Passo Posporcora, the Val Fiorenza and the Pian de Ra Spines. This path re-enters forest, crosses a stream and climbs steadily to the pass (1711 m); look up left to view a WW1 military ruin. From here the path makes a long zigzagging descent to the Pian de ra Spines. Eventually you turn right onto a broad track (#417) which follows above the right bank of the Boite and reaches a minor road at the Olympia camping ground at Fiames where you can catch a bus back to Cortina.*

WALK FIVE - DAY ONE - VALLE DE FANES (23 KM; 7.5 HRS)

This spectacular two-day walk gives you the chance to overnight in a charming mountain rifugio and to hike through the delightful Val di Fanes into the heart of the Dolomiti d'Ampezzo and Fanes-Sennes-Braies Nature Parks. Although not overly strenuous, the walk to Rifugio Fodara Vedla is long and mostly uphill so it is graded medium-difficult.

Take the local bus to Fiames and at the Albergo Fiames take the forest track north up valley (path #10) above the Torrente Boite and with great views of the Col Rosa and the Croda de R'Ancona. At Ponte Felizon, the main entrance to the Dolomiti d'Ampezzo Nature Park is reached. Continue on #10, signed to Val Travenanzes, ascending gently through woodland, crossing several side streams and the Rio di Fanes with views ahead of Taburlo and cross the Ponte Outo (Ladin for high) over the chasm. Soon after, the sure-footed should detour

Wary marmots can often be sighted in the higher valleys.

The Rio di Fanes sparkles in the summer sunshine.

right to the base of the Cascata di Fanes on an unmarked side path where fixed cables enable a short but dramatic cliff walk behind the waterfall. *Where the track bears left take the steep uphill short-cut path (W) signed to Alpe di Fanes, rejoining the track at Pian dai Sente. Continue up the valley and presently you reach a commemorative rock plaque which marks the Austrian 1916 front, at the Lago di Fanes.*

Past the lake, you cross the river and at the Pantane shrine you enter the Fanes-Sennes-Braies Nature Park. You are in alpine meadowland and ahead, the valley widens forming an amphitheatre beneath the imposing Monte

The steep ascent above Rifugio Pederü offers a rewarding view of the glacial Val di Rudo.

Vallon Bianco, named for its amazing white rock waves. *Presently, the route again follows the gushing stream and immediately before a footbridge, the short-cut path diverts right uphill on a WW1 muletrack. This boulder-strewn landscape is alive with marmots!* You regain the track just before a hairpin bend (now called path #10/11) which continues its ascent to the Lago di Limo (2159 m) and the Passo di Limo (2174 m) where vivid blue spring gentians abound in season. Below, the atmospheric karstic landscape of the Alpe di Fanes amphitheatre comes into view: the Lago Verde, the Rio San Viglio, the dairy huts of the Malga Fanes Piccola and the two rifugios situated nearby. *Descend steeply to the Rifugio Fanes (meals, accommodation), ideal for a late lunch. After feasting on the views, detour to the Lago Verde which feeds the Rio San Viglio and cross a footbridge (path #7/12) to the farm buildings and the Rifugio La Varella (meals, accommodation). From here, the route follows the Rio San Viglio (path #7) on a steeply descending jeep track to the Rifugio Pederü, a walk of 1.25 hr. From the rifugio, there is a very steep switchback ascent, initially on a former WW1 mule track (#7) and then on a forest path (#9), to reach Rifugio Fodara Vedla in another 1.25 hours. Alternatively, a 4WD taxi service operates between the four rifugios!* The long day's walk to overnight at this isolated but comfortable rifugio and *alpe* (alpine farm) is amply rewarded by the chance to watch the alpenglow on the surrounding mountains.

WALK FIVE - DAY TWO - L. DE FOSSES, V. DI GOTRES (18 KM; 7 HRS)

The return medium grade walk takes you on a less trodden path to the remote and magnificent setting of the Lago de Fosses before descending the delightful Val Salata and Val di Gotres. Before commencing, a short diversion (path #9) to the Lago de Fodera, surrounded by the peaks of the Lavinores and the Col Piera Maura, is worthwhile even if the lake is dry.

Ascend on the 4WD track (path #7) towards Rifugio Sennes and after 10 minutes diverge right onto a footpath marked 'Sennes' which crosses a high plain before rejoining the track to Sennes. The rifugio sits just above the often dry Lago de Sennes near where there is a quite bold colony of marmots. *Now take the 4WD track (#6) signed to Cortina (it continues down the Val Salata) and soon branch off up left (also on #6) on the track to Rifugio Biella. After some 2 km, you reach a signpost at Ota del Barancio (2190 m) where you divert down right onto an unnumbered footpath signed to Lago de Fosses. The path is narrow but easily followed.* It takes you through a dramatic amphitheatre scattered with white limestone boulders on the descent to the remote Lago de Fosses, set beneath the forbidding scree slopes of the Remeda Fossa. A lonely *malga* (farm) building guards the path junction near the lake and marmots are the area's main inhabitants.

At the malga, take path #26 signed to Malga Ra Stua/Croce del Gris, passing left of the Lago Piccolo on a boggy path and ascending above right of the Lago di Remeda Fossa before reaching Croce del Gris (2188 m). Pause here for the panoramic views which open out over the valley below. Continue on #26 signed to Campo Croce/Malga Ra Stua and soon begin the steep descent to the valley. Ahead you can see the 'main road' down valley. A preferable alternative is to

The farm buildings at Fodara Vedla catch the late afternoon light.

*The town of Cortina, with its
landmark church and dramatic
mountain backdrop.*

take the unnumbered footpath left across meadowland, just before the main track is reached, for Malga Ra Stua. Follow red-and-white waymarks, passing below a shrine and crossing two mountain streams before joining the road (#6) the short remaining distance to the Rifugio Malga Ra Stua where lunches are served (no accommodation).

From the rifugio, backtrack briefly up valley and take an unmarked (#8 on the map) forest track right uphill. At a signpost, take the right forking path (#8) signed to Forcella Lerosa/Val di Gotres. The path zigzags, winding uphill through beautiful woodland with venerable fir trees and abundant alpenrose. Every so often, memorable views back across the Alpe di Fannes open up and chances are good that you will see chamois from here onwards. Reaching the edge of meadowland, you turn right at a path junction following the track uphill. At the Forcella Lerosa (2020 m) the track becomes a 4WD track and begins a gentle descent through the Val di Gotres. About 2 km from the forcella a bridge crosses the Torrente Gotres after which you can detour briefly right to view an impressive cascade in the river. Reach a gate (with a turnstile!) and soon fork right onto a minor footpath (#8c) which drops steadily through forest, skirting right around a fenced-off military area and eventually reaching the main road (51) for a 1.25 km roadwalk right to the Rifugio Ospitale where you catch the bus to Cortina. Alternatively, backtrack slightly and find your way onto path #208 which follows below the road and from which you can exit at Ospitale.

NOTES ON THE DOLOMITES

TYPE OF WALK	Day walks from one base, plus one overnight walk
LENGTH OF WALK	96.25 kilometres (60 miles) over 6 days
DIFFICULTY	Varying from easy to medium-difficult
BASE	Cortina d'Ampezzo (population: 8000), set in a spectacular mountain basin

PUBLIC TRANSPORT
 Railway stations at Calalzo di Cadore (trains from Venice and Padua; Dolomiti Bus 30 from Calalzo to Cortina) and Dobbiaco (trains from Austria and Munich; SAD Bus 112 from Dobbiaco to Cortina).

CLIMATE
The climate is Alpine with long winters and heavy snows which can lie until July on exposed northern slopes. Weather conditions can change suddenly and vary with altitude. The walking season is from mid June to late September when the mountain refuges open; day walks are still viable into October.

MAP
Tabacco Carta Topografica per escursionisti No. 03: *Cortina d'Ampezzo E Dolomiti Ampezzani* 1:25,000
Note: a few paths have been renumbered; free 1:40,000 maps from the tourist office include these.

PATH
The walks are on non-vehicular roads and numbered footpaths, waymarked with red-and-white stripes.

ACCOMMODATION
Cortina's hotels are plentiful but many are expensive, particularly in the peak walking and skiing seasons. Enquire about half-pension rates. It is best to reserve beds in rifugios before setting out.

CUISINE
Cuisine is Venetian-influenced but with Tyrolean and Ladin accents. Polenta and risotto dishes are popular northern Italian first courses. Mountain trout is the main local fish, served grilled. Local game includes *capriolo* (roe deer). Apart from the ubiquitous wiener schnitzel, Tyrolean dishes include *knodelsuppe* (broth with bread dumplings), *spaetsli* (flour dumplings served with meat sauces) and *stinco* (roast veal or pork shank). In autumn, a wide array of wild mushrooms is available.

WILDLIFE
Ibex have been reintroduced into the Fanes-Sennes-Braies Nature Park (see Walk 4) and sightings of roe deer in forest and chamois above the treeline are common. Colonies of marmots are active from May to the first snowfalls; they can be identified by their piercing alarm cry. Capercaillie live in forest up to 1800 m, feeding on conifer needles and berries. Alpine wild flowers are abundant in season and include gentians, alpenrose, crocuses, Rhaetian poppies and orchids.

SPECIAL FEATURES
The dramatic falls at Cascata di Fanes; the almost lunar landscapes around Tre Cime di Lavaredo and Monte Lagazuoi; the high meadowlands of Val de Fanes, alpine tarns, the glacial Val Travenanzes.

FURTHER READING

WALKING IN THE DOLOMITES
by Gillian Price, published by Cicerone Press, UK, 1991

THE DOLOMITES OF ITALY: A TRAVEL GUIDE
by James and Anne Goldsmith, published by A & C Black, UK, 1989

USEFUL ADDRESSES

APT (TOURIST OFFICE)
Cortina d'Ampezzo, Tel: 0436) 3231   Fax: 0436) 3235   Email: apt1@sunrise.it

INTERNET SITE
http://www.sunrise.it/dolomiti (useful for accommodation)

THE CINQUE TERRE

A spectacular coastal and ridge walk linking the five impossibly pictur-esque fishing villages of the Cinque Terre and the sanctuaries, forests and terraced hillsides of the Apennine foothills.

The Cinque Terre or 'Five Lands' is an isolated strip of the Ligurian coast-line lying west of La Spezia and bounded by a mountainous hinterland, the edge of the Apennines. It is named after five small neighbouring villages–Monterosso al Mare, Vernazza, Corniglia, Manarola and Riomaggiore–which cling improbably to the rugged cliffs and hillsides that define this most striking landscape. Once accessible only by foot and by boat, the Cinque Terre villages still demand an approach on foot, the only way to appreciate their extraordinary setting as each one draws nearer, appearing and disap-pearing behind mountain spurs. Car-travellers are confronted with circui-tous mountain roads and are obliged to park at the perimeter of the traffic-free villages. Fortunately for the walker, a superb network of footpaths main-tained by the Club Alpino Italiano links all the villages and the hinterland hamlets and sanctuaries. Now waymarked and numbered, these ancient trails have been used for centuries by the villagers and farmers.

The origins of Corniglia and nearby Portovenere (where our walk com-mences) date back to the Roman Age while the other villages are younger, having been founded between the 8th and 11th centuries. The region's fortunes rose and fell with those of Genoa, the capital of Liguria and a once mighty mercantile and maritime power. Because of their strategic value to the Genoese, the villages were fortified in the 13th century and traces of this can still be seen. Inland, high above the coastal villages, perch a number of medieval sanctuaries which can be reached by side paths connecting the coast path to the parallel ridge path.

Although the recent advent of tourism has become an important part of the Cinque Terre's economy, the landscape, the villages and the people's way of life all appear remarkably unaffected by the 20th century. The tiny plots of arable land, terraced with dry-stone walls or *muretti*, continue to be worked by hand, the locals wander forest trails in search of mushrooms and the fishing boats are winched up each day from harbours so small there is no space for moorings. The intensively cultivated hillsides which separate each village produce small yields of olives for oil and grapes for the white Cinque Terre wines, most famously *sciacchetrà*, a rare blended desert wine.

The walk begins with this dramatic seascape, looking towards the Cinque Terre from Portovenere.

Cats also enjoy the relaxed lifestyle of the Cinque Terre.

This circular walk comprises four easy daily stages: there is no need to rush and every reason to linger. It takes the walker along the ridge top, to the sanctuaries, through forest and the remnant coastal vegetation above Portovenere and on the Punta Mesco. The walk also incorporates the entire *Sentiero Azzurro*, the classic coastal walk connecting the five Cinque Terre villages, with two nights spent in Vernazza, the most dramatic of the five. Be forewarned that you will undoubtedly share this coastal path with day walkers for the beauty of the Cinque Terre is no longer a secret. Accommodation in Vernazza is limited so you would be wise to reserve, particularly in summer. The short day stages mean that the walk is easily modified, for example to allow for different overnight stops. A final warning: sections of the coastal track are occasionally closed due to rock fall in which case a short train trip may be necessary; the local train emerges from its tunnel at each village and also stops at Levanto and La Spezia.

DAY ONE - PORTOVENERE TO VERNAZZA (17.5 KM; 7 HRS)

An ancient seafaring village, Portovenere today sits romantically beneath its castle, dividing the Cinque Terre promontory from the Gulf of La Spezia. In Roman times Portovenere (Portus Veneris) was a port for Roman galleys en route to Spain or Gaul. It was rebuilt as a fortified town in the 12th century by the Genoese who built the Castello Superiore (reconstructed in the 15th century) as a defence in the long wars between Genoa and Pisa. Old Portovenere is a narrow, single-street town, entered through an archway in the walls which descend from the castle. The tall houses squeezed between street and sea were originally built as defensive towers and face inwards. Spectacularly sited on high cliffs at the very end of the promontory stands the church of San Pietro with its black and white facade. It was built in Genoese-Gothic style in the 13th century, supposedly on the site of

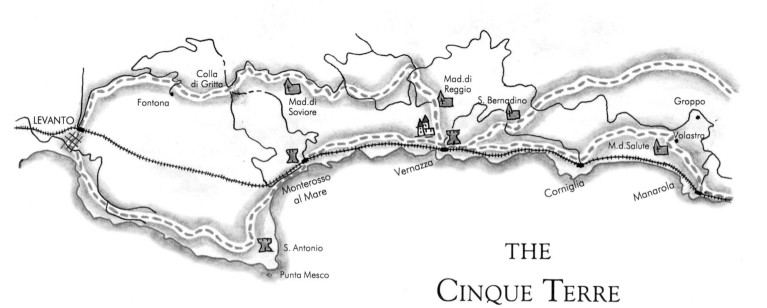

THE
CINQUE TERRE

a temple dedicated to Venus. The 12th century Romanesque church of San Lorenzo in the upper town bears an unusual carving depicting the saint's martyrdom, roasted alive on a grill.

Our journey begins in the Piazza Bastreri at a signboard just outside the village gateway. The route, waymarked with horizontal red and white stripes, is the CAI path #1, the *Sentiero Rosso*, a ridge walk following the watershed between coast and hinterland. Buy lunch supplies before leaving, or dine at the trattoria at Colle del Telegrafo. *Initially the path climbs steeply, skirting the castle walls.* In fair weather you will have magnificent views over the Gulf of la Spezia to the Apennines and looking SE, a wonderful view of San Pietro and the island of Palmaria. *Continue on #1 to meet a minor road at a hairpin. Follow this past an old quarry, diverge right to short-cut a bend and rejoin the road for 500 m. At a sign which warns of wild boar hunting, the path leaves the road to follow a spur high above the rocky coast providing dramatic coastal views.* This part of the walk is probably the most difficult and care should be taken negotiating it. *Further on, the path touches another road at a bend and continues through forest, rejoining the road briefly before reaching the medieval village of Campiglia at the church of Santa Caterina.*

Through Campiglia (ignore branch paths 4/a, 4/b and 11), path 1 leaves the road at a crossroads and climbs left up stairs through some outlying dwellings and continues to ascend a steep ridge through chestnut woodland before levelling. Walk through the Palestra nel Verde, a forest gymnasium replete with assorted wooden exercise paraphernalia and pass a building that serves as both chapel (San Antonio) and bar (La Bignetta) before briefly joining a road near the junction with #4. Leave the road, forking left to reach Colle del Telegrafo, an hour

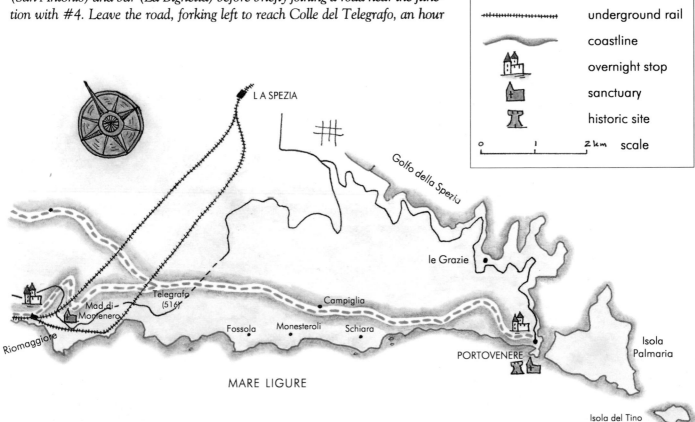

LEGEND

route of walk

road

underground rail

coastline

overnight stop

sanctuary

historic site

0   1   2 km   scale

L A SPEZIA

Golfo della Spezia

le Grazie

Telegrafo (516)

Campiglia

Mad. di Montenero

Fossola

Monesteroli

Schiara

Riomaggiore

PORTOVENERE

Isola Palmaria

MARE LIGURE

Isola del Tino

Vernazza's Belforte tower (above) overlooks the tiny harbour (below).

from Campiglia, where #3 and 3/a and three roads all converge and where there is a trattoria. Leaving the road, you ascend slightly on #1, now a foot track, with fine views of the Cinque Terre coast. The path continues through chestnut forest, eventually becoming an unsealed vehicular track which is followed for 1.5 km. Near la Croce, ignore the #01 junction but take care to diverge left from the vehicular track hereabouts to continue along the ridge's crest. Pass the junction with #02; soon after, a sign points right to a nearby menhir (standing stone) which stands no longer. The path now starts to descend through beech and chestnut and then through more open bracken to a clearing where #7/a forks left down to Corniglia. Here you take the sharp right path signed #1 to Levanto. In five minutes, at the Cigoletta saddle, #7 joins from the right, coincides briefly with #1 and then forks left, signposted to Vernazza.

Take path #7 which initially lacks waymarkings, and descends mostly as a broad stony path to reach a minor road just past a camping area. Cross the road and descend steeply on a very narrow waymarked path to reach the main road. The path, now overgrown, is picked up on the other side of the road. It descends to touch a minor road at a hairpin bend and continues a zigzagging descent first as a broad, loose track and then as a narrow footpath to reach steps which come out beside the church of San Bernardino. Behind the church, climb the stairs between the hamlet's buildings, then wend through a vineyard where there are excellent views of the steep terracing covering the nearby hills. The path soon weaves down to a road after turning left beside a stone wall. Turn left and cross to a narrow footpath continuing uphill and soon levelling. Here you join a lane for a short distance before veering off right on another minor path high above the water. Though close, Vernazza remains obscured behind a rocky spur. The path zigzags very steeply down the hillside, eventually joining the coastal path #2, the Sentiero Azzurro. Turn right to continue the steep descent into Vernazza. The views over Vernazza and towards Monterosso are exquisite. Allow 4 hours from Colle del Telegrafo to Vernazza.

Vernazza is possibly the most dramatic and beautiful of the Cinque Terre villages. Tall pastel-coloured houses tumble down the promontory to Vernazza's tiny harbour and breakwater, overlooked by the ruined tower of the Castello Belforte, a reminder of the port's importance to the 13th century Genoan Republic. Colourful boats adorn both harbour and Vernazza's main pedestrian street where many are accommodated. A maze of paths and stairways (*arpaie*) connect the houses with the street. Vernazza boasts a choice of restaurants, bars, small hotels and private rooms (ask at a bar).

DAY TWO - VERNAZZA TO LEVANTO (9 KM; 4 HRS) & RETURN

Today's route to Levanto via Monterosso and the Punta Mesco follows some of Liguria's most spectacular coastline and requires two steep ascents. If you plan to walk back to Vernazza, lunch should be had in Levanto; otherwise, the ruins above the Punta Mesco make an idyllic picnic spot.

The Sentiero Azzurro path #2 leaves Vernazza's main street up stairs then on a steep path beside the church of Santa Margherita d'Antiochia. The path climbs high above the sea, providing wonderful vistas back over Vernazza to

Many sanctuaries such as the Madonna di Montenero command sweeping views.

Corniglia and beyond, all framed by sea cliffs and the deep blue of the Ligurian Sea. The narrow path levels and you pass through tiny terraced plots and nego-tiate narrow bridges over rushing streams as the path descends to Monterosso in a zigzagging series of stone steps. Allow 1hr 45min for this leg of the walk. Monterosso's two beaches are divided by a small headland which also serves to separate the old town from the new. Sited on fairly level land, Monterosso has grown in recent years to accommodate the needs of tourism. You should visit the 16th century Capucchin convent to view a Crucifixion, possibly painted by the Flemish master Van Dyck. The elegant lines of the church of San Giovanni Battista, built in Genoese-Gothic style, should also be admired. On the headland, the 13th century Torre Aurora (Dawn Tower), a remnant of fortifications, is now undercut by a road tunnel.

Once through the road tunnel, the walk continues as path #10 along the waterfront towards the large rock sculpture 'il Gigante' (depicting the god Nep-tune) and the restaurant of the same name. Climb the steep steps behind the restaurant and briefly join a road which you leave at a bend to climb more steps on a path to Punta Mesco. As you climb, the views back along the Cinque Terre are ever more extensive. Where #10 joins #1, detour left for some 200 m to perhaps picnic among the evocative ruins of the Eremo San Antonio and the old semaforo *(beacon) with breathtaking ocean views in both direc-tions. Back at the junction, keep left, taking path #1 on which it is 5 km of gradual descent to reach Levanto. Initially the path is through unspoiled forest providing filtered views; eventually you join a minor road to Levanto and then continue on a path between the road and the sea. Path becomes stairway, passing beneath a 13th century castle and wending its way down to the sea promenade.*

You may not wish to linger in Levanto, a fading seaside resort lacking the charm of its Cinque Terre neighbours. *To return to Vernazza by train, head inland along Levanto's main street, Corso Roma, for 1 km to reach the station.* Alternatively, you could walk back to Vernazza the same way but, if time permits, the recommended route is inland on paths #12, 1 and 8 for some 8.5 km via the sanctuaries of the Madonna di Soviore and the Madonna di Reggio above Monterosso and Vernazza.

Path #12 commences a few hundred metres inland from the station and follows a minor road initially NE, parallel with the Torrent Ghiararo, later swinging SE continuing to follow the road towards Fontona, leaving it to short-cut several hairpin bends. As the road climbs there are wonderful views of Levanto and of the numerous little hill towns dotting the hinterland. The road stops at Fontona, path #12 continuing SE to reach the Monterosso road at Colla di Gritta where #1 is picked up. Path #1 follows a minor road for 2 km to the Santuario della Madonna di Soviore. Soviore is Liguria's most ancient sanctuary, built in the 9th century and modified from the 13th century on. Its magnificent ogival portal and rose window make a contrast with its facade and the square next to the sanctuary provides an excellent viewpoint. *The forest route from Soviore to the Foce Drignana on #1 is straightforward. Here you exit the woods at a junction to turn right onto a minor road, following #8 for Vernazza.* Half way to Vernazza you reach the 11th century Santuario della Madonna di Reggio with its linear facade sheltering the black Madonna known locally as 'l'Africana'. *The scenic descent to Vernazza now follows a broad, stone-laid path which is used for pilgrimages to the sanctuary.*

DAY THREE - VERNAZZA TO RIOMAGGIORE (8 KM; 4 HRS)

There is more spectacular coastal scenery on today's journey as the three remaining Cinque Terre villages are discovered on a combination of the Sentiero Azzurro and a less trodden inland route through the hilltown of Volastra and its sanctuary. The suggested lunch destination is Manarola.

Leave Vernazza on path #2, ascending the narrow laneways you descended on Day 1 and pausing often for the stunning views back down to Vernazza and the coast beyond. After climbing steeply, the path meanders more gently through some of the Cinque Terre's most photogenic olive groves. The buildings of Prevo are passed and the path begins its descent towards Corniglia. Corniglia sits atop a rocky pinnacle, terraced vines cascading down its slopes, and commands superb views of the other towns. Unlike the other four harbour villages, Corniglia is a true hilltown, its origin lying in farming not fishing. It is also the most isolated and appears the least touched by modernity.

Our route bypasses the centre of Corniglia, to which a detour should be made, and passes behind the church of San Pietro, built in 1334. Soon, at a path junction, turn left uphill on the narrow path #7/a for Volastra. After 30 min-

Bold Mediterranean colours are used liberally along the Ligurian coast.

utes' steep climbing through woodland, the path forks; take the path right signposted #6/d to Volastra. It soon levels and runs roughly parallel with the coast along muretti which divide the olive groves and vines. Through this unique manmade landscape Corniglia can be seen receding far below. Volastra is reached at the Santuario di Madonna della Salute, about 1.5 hr from Corniglia. The church possesses a fine portal and mullion window lending elegance to its facade although the interior has suffered from unfortunate alterations. The path goes through the church grounds, down a street through the village and continues the descent (now waymarked as #6) out of Volastra on a beautiful stone-laid path through more picturesque olive groves. Cross the Manarola road and rejoin it to descend to Manarola's outskirts. To reach the harbour, walk past the fine 14th century Gothic church of San Lorenzo and cross over the railway line to continue down the main pedestrian street. Perched like Vernazza on the side of a rock spur, Manarola's picturesque waterfront comprises a tiny harbour protected by a breakwater and a well-fenced promenade high above the crashing surf. Vine-terraced hills form the backdrop to the staggered lines of tall pastel buildings crowding the harbour. Take time to enjoy Manarola because Riomaggiore is less than 30 minutes away on the final section of the Sentiero Azzurro, the so-called Via dell'Amore or Lovers' Lane.

Return over the railway line and go right through the pedestrian tunnel parallel with the line to reach Manarola's station. Then climb the steps behind the station to reach the Via dell'Amore. This level cliffside walkway has been

The quintessential fishing village of Manarola seems to encrust its rocky spur.

A 15th century fresco decorates the gateway to old Portovenere.

rebuilt after landslides: it is heavily concreted and roofed for protection from rock fall. Despite its name, this most famous section of the coastal walk is probably the dullest. *Riomaggiore station is soon reached and then another pedestrian tunnel which exits at the village.* Riomaggiore, relatively accessible by road and so popular with visitors, has several hotels and many private rooms. Make sure you explore its tiny harbour, south of the station.

DAY FOUR - RIOMAGGIORE TO PORTOVENERE (13.5 KM; 4.5 HRS)

The return to Portovenere via Madonna di Montenero retraces some of the scenic highlights of the Sentiero Rosso. Lunch could be had at the trattoria at the Colle del Telegrafo if a late start is contemplated, otherwise buy lunch supplies in Riomaggiore.

Leave Riomaggiore on path #3, ascending the main street to reach the carpark on its outskirts. You then reach the road which is crossed, the path continuing uphill and following the course of the Valle di Riomaggiore. Still ascending, the path crosses the main road after which it loops back (SSW) and reaches the Santuario della Madonna di Montenero, a beautiful church which now houses a restaurant. The church square offers a wonderful panorama extending from the Punta Mesco to the islands off Portovenere. *From here the path continues to climb and soon forks; ignore the left fork (#3/a) and continue to climb on #3.* The changing views back over the church to the coast are worth several pauses. *The path eventually emerges at the Colle del Telegrafo junction just in front of the trattoria. From here you return on path #1 to Portovenere as described in Day 1.* A longer variant between Telegrafo and Campiglia could involve leaving path #1 for an exploration of the isolated hamlets of Fossola, Monesteroli and Schiara, from each of which steep steps lead to the sea where sandy beaches and wild, rocky cliffs can be explored. This option would rejoin the main path at Campiglia.

NOTES ON THE CINQUE TERRE

TYPE OF WALK   Circular

LENGTH OF WALK   48 kilometres (30 miles); four days

DIFFICULTY   An easy grade walk with one fairly long day and many short ascents

START & FINISH   Portovenere, a picturesque fishing village of Roman origins

PUBLIC TRANSPORT
FS train to La Spezia from Genoa or Pisa and then an ATC bus from La Spezia to Portovenere. Local trains connect La Spezia with Levanto and the five Cinque Terre villages.

LUGGAGE   Excess luggage may be stored for a sizeable fee at La Spezia Centrale railway station.

CLIMATE
Protected by mountains from extremes of cold, coastal Liguria enjoys a mild Mediterranean climate. Year-round walking is possible. Rainfall is quite high, especially in late autumn.

MAP
Club Alpino Italiano (CAI) *Cinque Terre e Parco di Montemarcello* 1:40,000
or Kompass No. 644 *Cinque Terre* 1:50,000 (with inset street maps of villages)
or Edizioni Multigraphic *Cinque Terre, Golfo della Spezia, Montemarcello* 1:25,000

PATH   Entirely on waymarked and numbered footpaths including the *Sentieri Rosso* and *Azzurro*.

SHORTER VARIANT   (see Days 1, 2 & 3)
A two-day version: *Bus from La Spezia to Portovenere;* 1 - ridge walk from Portovenere to Vernazza; 2 - *train to Monterosso;* coast walk from Monterosso to Riomaggiore; *train to La Spezia.*

VILLAGES
Portovenere (population 2000), Campiglia (150), **Vernazza** (800), Monterosso (1600), Levanto (5700), Corniglia (250), Volastra (180), Manarola (570), **Riomaggiore** (1500).

ACCOMMODATION   Portovenere hotels are somewhat expensive. Vernazza and Riomaggiore both have cheaper hotels as well as private rooms.

CUISINE
Liguria is famous for its *pesto*, a sauce of olive oil, basil, garlic, pine nuts and parmesan cheese. Seafood is ubiquitous here and is uniformly excellent whether in in a *zuppa di pesce*, pasta dishes, *risotto* or grilled simply, in the Ligurian manner. *Tian Vernazza* is a local specialty, a gratin of potatoes, tomatoes and anchovies. Fresh forest mushrooms appear on autumn menus. The Cinque Terre produces its own white wine, including the sweet and luscious *sciacchetrà*, drunk with dessert or as a digestif.

WILDLIFE
Large animals are scarce as a result of hunting and intense cultivation; signs warn of wild boar hunting from October onwards. The waters off the Cinque Terre were recently designated as a marine reserve and a number of whale and dolphin species frequent these waters.

SPECIAL FEATURES
Portovenere and the Golfo della Spezia; the five picturesque Cinque Terre villages; spectacular coastal scenery from Punta Mesco; the steeply terraced vineyards and olive groves; the inland sanctuaries.

USEFUL ADDRESSES

APT (TOURIST OFFICE)
19100 La Spezia, Viale G. Mazzini, 47; Tel: 0187) 770900; Fax: 0187) 770908
Branch office: Piazza Bastreri 7, 19025 Portovenere Tel: 0187) 790691 Fax: 0187) 790215

INTERNET SITES   http://www.cinqueterre.it   http://www.portovenere.it

THE HIGH BLACK FOREST

A leisurely walk through the charming southern Black Forest where romantic forest paths provide easy access to glacial lakes, mountain summits, cascading streams and fertile valleys dotted with traditional farmhouses.

The Black Forest or *Schwarzwald* is not a single forest as such; it refers to an extensive region in the extreme southwest of Germany where forest predominates, covering the ridges, and is broken up by the verdant pasture and arable farmland of the valley floors. Nor is the forest original, rather it is woodland which has been managed for hundreds of years like almost all of Europe's remaining forest. Neither circumstance detracts from the Black Forest's beauty and its popularity as a walking destination. Once you've seen the mists which at times shroud the dense canopy of trees, it is easy to understand how this came to be a land of legends and poetry.

The Black Forest has a long history of settlement. The Celts who settled here were subsequently conquered by the Romans, who built forest roads and observation towers and availed themselves of the abundant thermal springs in and around Baden-Baden. Some outstanding Benedictine and Cistercian monasteries and abbeys are a testament to the region's early Christianisation, originally by Irish missionaries in the 7th century. The Cistercians are to be thanked for developing the local viticulture. Not surprisingly, the timber industry has been of longstanding importance. Wood was used for ships' masts, for paper and furniture-making, for wood carving and, from the 17th century, for the world famous Black Forest clock industry. Huge quantities of wood were also needed to make the charcoal which was essential for glassmaking. Winemaking (including liqueurs), glassblowing and woodworking are still important to the local economy.

The Southern or High Black Forest (*Hochschwarzwald*) is a large granite massif which rises up to the east of the Rhine plain, carved by deep east-west valleys. This is the most mountainous part of the Black Forest and was long the most inaccessible. Though not comparable with the peaks of the nearby Alps, its highest mountains provide wonderful panoramas from their rounded summits. Fir, elm and pine woods comprise over half of the Black Forest but these are interspersed with areas of deciduous species ensuring an autumn show of colour. Much of the landscape has been designated nature reserve or 'protected landscape', keeping at bay the incursion of motorways and other modern blights. This has been due in large

In the Black Forest, clumps of dense forest are interspersed with rolling pasture.

THE HIGH BLACK FOREST

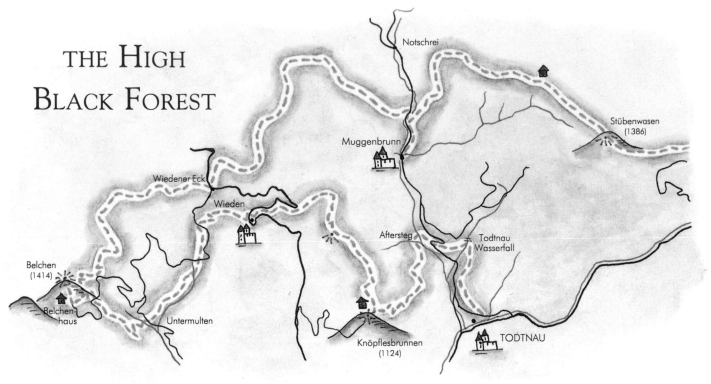

Traditional Black Forest farmhouses have large roofs, under which hay is stored.

part to the *Schwarzwaldverein* (the Black Forest Society), Germany's oldest walking organisation, which since 1864 has fought against inappropriate development to protect the Black Forest's culture and environment.

Thanks also to the Schwarzwaldverein, the Black Forest is one of Europe's oldest and best known walking areas, with 23000 km of waymarked footpaths. The 281 km Westweg, one of three high-level walks traversing the Black Forest from north to south, is Europe's first waymarked long distance footpath, dating from 1900. Our gentler five-day walk is more circuitous and takes in many of the high points, in both senses, of the High Black Forest. It starts in picturesque Bärental at Germany's highest railway station and ends only a day's walk away at the lovely village of Todtnau. Between times, the walk is centred on Feldberg and Belchen, the Black Forest's highest and third highest peaks, and on the delightful landscapes and mountain villages which surround them. The extraordinary network of footpaths makes it easy to vary this fine walk while the region's famed hospitality and cuisine will undoubtedly add to your enjoyment.

DAY ONE - BARENTAL TO HINTERZARTEN (11.5 KM; 4 HRS)

Today's short walk provides a gentle introduction to the journey. From Bärental, the way descends gradually to the lovely waters of Titisee and follows its eastern shore to reach Titisee township from where forest paths lead up to an exquisite viewpoint over Hinterzarten, the day's destination.

Bärental is a small village which is disproportionately popular with hikers as it is the closest railway station to the Feldberg. It is advisable to reserve a room during peak walking season. *The path begins at the far end of*

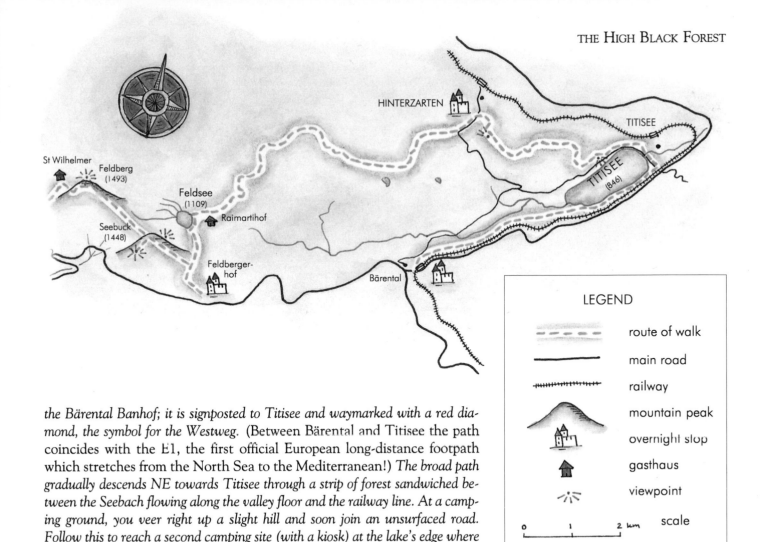

LEGEND

- route of walk
- main road
- railway
- mountain peak
- overnight stop
- gasthaus
- viewpoint
- scale 0 1 2 km

the Bärental Banhof; it is signposted to Titisee and waymarked with a red diamond, the symbol for the Westweg. (Between Bärental and Titisee the path coincides with the E1, the first official European long-distance footpath which stretches from the North Sea to the Mediterranean!) *The broad path gradually descends NE towards Titisee through a strip of forest sandwiched between the Seebach flowing along the valley floor and the railway line. At a camping ground, you veer right up a slight hill and soon join an unsurfaced road. Follow this to reach a second camping site (with a kiosk) at the lake's edge where you should pause to enjoy the marvellous views, then continue through the site. The path hugs the lake's edge for about 1.5 km before reaching a* gasthaus *on a minor road. This curves around some distance from the water's edge, offering wonderful views down the lake. From here the path heads NW into Titisee township on Seestrasse, the lakeside promenade.* Set at the end of Germany's most beautiful and probably best-known glacial lake, Titisee receives throngs of visitors and conferees. Boat tours depart from Seestrasse or you can ply the waters in a rented paddleboat.

The Westweg is left behind at Titisee. Turn left to follow the lake's western shore and, just after the swimming pool, cross the road to turn right uphill onto a grassy track waymarked with a red cross on yellow background and signposted to Hinterzarten. Where the fence on your left ends, turn sharp left and follow a path uphill. The path veers right after a house and zigzags up through the pines. It joins a minor road at the hamlet of Bühlhof, with good views down to Titisee. Turn left onto the road and soon divert right on a path uphill (red cross). Pass to the left of a camping site and turn left uphill at a T-junction. The path now leaves the open pasture for the forest and soon forks; take the left fork, waymarked with a blue circle, for Hinterzarten. Keep on this until you reach a stone cross where you veer right into the pines on the blue circle path for Hinterzarten. Eventually you come to a clearing from where there are distant views of the peaks of Seebuck and Feldberg. Presently the forest path reaches the edge of the ridge at the top of

*The sparkling waters of Titisee
on a clear autumn day.*

a ski jump. Walk behind this to reach Scheibenfelsen Aussicht, a superb viewpoint overlooking Hinterzarten and beyond. Descend the steep gravel path alongside the ski jump to reach a lane beside Hinterzarten's cemetery.

Hinterzarten is a stylish mountain resort set, along with its neighbouring hamlets, amidst verdant farmland. Unusually it features a large village green which is surrounded by elegant hotels and a baroque Catholic church. Hinterzarten has a variety of accommodation as well as a tourist office.

DAY TWO - HINTERZARTEN TO FELDBERGER-HOF (10.5 KM; 4 HRS)

On today's journey to the base of the Feldberg you are rarely far from one of the wild streams which drain the mountain's flanks. The route is through forest of exceptional beauty and culminates in a visit to Feldsee, a hidden glacial lake.

Leave Hinterzarten from the signboard near the Catholic church. Turn towards pasture land and cross the Zartenbach. Immediately turn left onto a path following the stream until you reach the Erlenbrucker Strasse. Turn right uphill onto this road, passing the ski museum Hugenhof. Turn right on a lane up to the hotel Sonnenberg, below which commences the Emil-Thoma-Weg, waymarked with a green circle. Take this gravel path to enter some of the most enchanting woodland you will encounter on this walk. The path passes a dam on the left and ascends gently between moss-covered rock and dense forest. Presently you reach a turn-off left signed to Mathislesweiher, a forest lake which is worth a short detour. Otherwise go straight on, cross a track, join an unsealed road and, after the farm Am Feldberg, turn left (SE) onto Rufenhofstrasse signposted to Feldberg. Cross a bridge over a mountain stream and take the right-hand track uphill, marked Emil-Thoma-Weg. At a five-way-intersection where there is a shelter, take the forest track waymarked with a yellow circle, signed to Raimartihof/ Feldsee. Cross two streams and then leave the forest track, taking a footpath right uphill into the woods at a point marked Raimartihof/Feldsee Gasthaus. Turn left onto a broader track continuing uphill and soon reach the gasthaus.

Set amidst the Raimartihof farmland, the gasthaus is a welcome spot to buy lunch; Feldsee, however, is the place to eat a picnic lunch if the weather is good. *From the gasthaus, take the Karl-Egon-Weg, waymarked with a red circle and signed to Feldsee.* The highlight of the day's walk, Feldsee can only be reached by foot and is protected within the largest nature reserve in Baden-Württemberg. This small glacial lake (32.6 m deep and 300 m or so wide) of great beauty is surrounded by forest and by a high amphitheatre of rock walls over which cascade the streams which feed it. A path circles the lake and on the far side is a narrow beach where swimming would be possible (signs prohibit swimming on the near side). *After circling the lake, rejoin the waymarked path, heading right uphill through beautiful woodland. The path now zigzags steeply uphill; look back occasionally for the views as Feldsee recedes. Eventually, at a path junction, you reach the base of the Feldberg chairlift.* Walk down the road to reach Feldberger-hof or nearby Hebelhof, popular downhill ski areas where accommodation is available.

The village of Hinterzarten from the Scheibenfelsen Aussicht.

Day Three - Feldberger-hof to Muggenbrunn (14 km; 4.5 hrs)

From Feldberger-hof there is a choice of routes up to Feldberg and you could take the chairlift part way. Be warned that Feldberg itself is not overly attractive; the area was deforested for pasture in the 18th and 19th centuries and the added communications and skiing infrastructure are not things of great beauty. *For the suggested route return to the base of the chairlift and take the gravel path which climbs to its right. This steep path follows close to the forest edge and reaches a monument to Bismark shortly after the upper station of the chairlift.* This point affords a bird's-eye view of Feldsee and beyond. *Detour left on a short path marked to Seebuck where you can ascend the television tower for a near-circular panorama (Feldberg's summit obscures the Vosges). Return to the monument and veer left on the path (red circle) on the saddle approach to Feldberg. There is a path junction at Grüblesattel where the Feldberg road is briefly joined; you are now back on the Westweg (red diamond) which leads to Feldberg's 1493 m summit.* This offers wonderful views of Titisee, the Hochfirst and, on very clear days, the Schwäbische Alb and the Randen. From the west side of the summit is a view over the Wiesental.

Retrace your steps briefly and turn right onto Westweg for a descent to St Wilhelmer Hutte where refreshments may be bought. Follow the road downhill and at a hairpin bend leave it to follow a forest path W, still on the waymarked Westweg, towards Stübenwasen (1386 m). This is a nature reserve, protecting alpine flora and chamois (there is a detailed signboard in German). The

Feldsee, a glacial lake hidden below the peak of Feldberg.

The peak of Belchen is a deservedly popular viewpoint.

A couple of the denizens of the Black Forest.

path veers NW and descends gently to the Stübenwasen inn. From here the path crosses and briefly rejoins a forest road before veering off right. After 1.5 km you join a road in the direction of Notschrei for 600 m. Turn right (S) onto a forest path which soon reaches another minor road. Here you leave the Westweg which follows the road to Notschrei. To reach Muggenbrunn, you follow the road the other way and very soon turn right (S) onto another forest road which, after about 1.5 km, comes out at the main L124 road. Continue south on this to reach the village of Muggenbrunn in less than a kilometre.

DAY FOUR - MUGGENBRUNN TO WIEDEN (20 KM; 6.5 HRS)

Today's journey is by far the longest, allowing for an ascent of Belchen, the most beautiful of the region's peaks with its stunning views. From there you descend to Wieden through postcard scenery. Alternatively, Belchen can be reached less strenuously by bus from the road above Wieden. Buy lunch provisions before starting or else dine at the Wiedener Eck hotel.

From Muggenbrunn, retrace your steps to where you joined the L124 at the end of yesterday's walk. Continue on the road for a further 200 m, crossing the Langenbach, and take the next road left, waymarked with a yellow ring. After 1.7 km, leave the road at a bend and turn right onto a forest path, heading NW uphill. In 500 m you come to a path junction with a signpost where you turn left; you are now back on the Westweg. Turn left onto a broad track briefly and then right immediately after onto another forest path. Soon you join a road heading SW and where the road ends, continue ahead on a track, presently passing a shelter and skirting farmland. Soon you leave the forest and cross pasture, with delightful views down the valley. Pass a large farmhouse and go through a wire gate to soon re-enter the forest, finally emerging at a road junction at the Wiedener Eck mountain hotel. Wiedener Eck (1050 m), overlooking the village of Wieden and its neighbouring hamlets, is on the Münstertal-Schönau mountain pass and is surrounded by superb scenery. Over the road is an information board for booking accommodation in the Wieden area.

Across the other road opposite the hotel is a nature reserve sign from where you take the Westweg, marked to Belchen. The ascent of Belchen is constant but not overly steep, mainly on forest trails and footpaths. *After passing beneath a ski-lift you get a commanding view of scenic Münstertal to the north, making for a good picnic spot. The route leaves the road and passes beneath a second ski-lift, rejoins a road briefly, leaving it to climb and contour around Heidstein. The summit of Belchen soon comes into view ahead. Cross a gravel road at Krinne (there is water, a table and shelter 50 m left up the road) where you follow a footpath W uphill. The path contours around a hill then zigzags more steeply to reach a roadside clearing where there are lovely easterly views. Still on the Westweg, the path climbs steeply, zigzagging to gain the last 200 m in altitude. At a granite post marking a crosspath, take the highest path to soon reach Belchen's rounded summit (1414 m).* The cleared summit has an observation table and panoramic views of the deep cut Münstertal and Wiesental valleys and the tiny hamlets dotting the landscape. If visibility is good, the Alps of the Bernese Oberland can be seen and, much closer, the Rhine river plain and the rounded High Vosges of Alsace.

Descend on one of the paths to nearby Belchenhaus, a gasthaus by the bus stop at the end of the road. A well-earned afternoon tea is in order before the return to Wieden. *Take the blue diamond path from in front of Belchenhaus signed to Wiedener Eck via Obermulten and Lückle. This crosses open land then zigzags down through forest, crosses the Belchen road and continues downhill soon turning sharp right. At a path junction, keep left (blue diamond). Cross a broad forest track and, at another junction, take the leftmost path downhill (leaving the blue diamond path). Turn left downhill where it joins a broad forest road and at a clearing with a stream turn sharp right downhill on the path signed Multen/Wiedener Eck. Soon turn left onto a gravel road signed to Multen/Lückle. At the Belchen Multen Pension, follow the road downhill briefly and then turn left on a lane to Lückle/Wiedener Eck. This follows a stream along a particularly photogenic valley. Cross the stream and follow the road above the stream's other bank. At the end of the cleared valley take the right fork uphill to Wiedener Eck. Cross the main road at the parking bay at Lückle and continue straight ahead on a path marked Wieden/Wiedener Eck. Presently the path forks (the upper path is to Wiedener Eck) so take the lower right path which crosses the road and zigzags down through farmland to reach the charming village of Wieden.*

DAY FIVE - WIEDEN TO TODTNAU (11 KM; 4.5 HRS)

Today's route follows the course of a mountain stream as you climb out of the Wieden valley and along a panoramic ridge to Knöpflesbrunnen. The highlight is perhaps the impressive cascades of the Todtnauer Wasserfall.

Leave from the church in the centre of Wieden, crossing the park and the Wiedenbach and taking the road up behind the supermarket. When the path divides, take the fork signed Knöpflesbrunnen, continuing around a small cemetery. Through delightful farmland, the path crosses another stream and contours right around a hill. At a farmhouse there is a path junction: continue uphill to reach the road where there is a sign to Knöpflesbrunnen. Follow the road briefly to a hairpin bend and veer right onto a lane. The footpath soon diverges off right through elms, following above the lovely waldbach (forest stream). Keep left on this path and then cross a bridge. The path skirts the edge of the forest and soon zigzags up to a seat and viewpoint where a sign points to Knöpflesbrunnen. Follow a broad track which climbs uphill through open land and, shortly after a hairpin bend, turn right uphill on a narrow footpath marked Knöpflesbrunnen and Dachsrein. Turn left at a sharp bend and walk through a narrow tunnel of fir trees. Soon turn right onto a wide, possibly muddy, track signed Panoramaweg/Knöpflesbrunnen. True to name the road follows a ridge, providing fine views below over the Wieden valley. Continue on for 2 km to a T-junction at Hasbacher Höhe. Turn right and follow this minor road, waymarked with a blue diamond, which soon leaves the forest, passes a large cross on a spire on the left and reaches the Knöpflesbrunnen Gasthaus where lunch can be bought. For another panoramic viewpoint, you should make the brief detour to the Knöpflesbrunnen summit by taking a footpath right from the road just after the gasthaus.

From the gasthaus, return to the signpost and take the right-hand path signed to Todtnau (blue diamond). Proceed downhill through woods, across a gravel road and onto another gravel road, turning left for Todtnau. Turn right downhill

The mists which occasionally shroud the High Black Forest add a note of mystery.

*The dramatic Todtnauer Wasserfall
in its woodland setting.*

on the blue diamond path, cutting off a loop in the road. The path rejoins the road at a bend where there is a shelter and fireplace. Leave the waymarked route and take the road downhill through meadowland to reach the hamlet of Hasbach after which you veer right onto a footpath which joins a lower road into Aftersteg after 400 m. Once in the village, turn right to pass the church, cross the Schönenbach, and pass the Rathaus to reach the L126 road at a hairpin bend. Continue straight on uphill on the main road to pass the Gläsblaserhof. A visit is recommended for a glassblowing demonstration. Just after the Gläsblaserhof, veer right off the main road onto a lower gravel road which becomes a broad path signposted 'wasserfall'. The viewpoint beneath the Todtnauer Wasserfall is reached after a delightful 500 m forest walk. In spate it is an impressive sight and sound as the torrent tumbles dramatically 100 m over a series of cascades. Below the main viewpoint you can detour to follow the torrent on a path which switches from bank to bank over a series of sometimes slippery wooden bridges. Back at the viewpoint, cross the bridge and continue in the same direction on the blue diamond path. This now descends through pretty forest for 2 km to Todtnau. At a path junction (750 m spot height) the path zigzags down a steep slope, leaving the forest to reach the church in the upper town.

Set in the upper Wiesental, Todtnau is a thriving and particularly attractive Black Forest town. Its centre has been spared the ravages of many ski resort towns, its well-preserved, pastel buildings lining the *marktplatz*. Todtnau is compact yet large enough to boast all the amenities. From here, you can return to Bärental by bus or you could take a full day to walk there, rejoining the Westweg and ascending the Herzogenhorn (1415 m), the Black Forest's second highest peak.

NOTES ON THE HIGH BLACK FOREST

TYPE OF WALK   One-way (can be made circular with an extra day's walking)

LENGTH OF WALK   67 kilometres (42 miles); five days

DIFFICULTY   An easy walk, with a longer route on the fourth day

START   Bärental, in the shadow of the Feldberg

FINISH   Todtnau, a delightful Schwartzwald mountain town

PUBLIC TRANSPORT
Train from Freiberg on the Dortmund/Mainz/Basel line to Feldberg Bärental. SüdbadenBus from Todtnau to Freiberg Hauptbahnhof or to Feldberg Bärental Bahnhof.

LUGGAGE
Leave excess luggage at Freiberg Hauptbahnhof or else at Bärental if returning there.

CLIMATE   Winters can be long (November to April) with heavy snowfall. July and August are warm and dry. Ideal walking seasons are late spring/early summer and early autumn, especially September.

MAP   Landesvermessungsamt Baden-Württemberg No. 25 *Feldberg Belchen Schluchsee* 1:35,000

PATH   Minor surfaced and unsurfaced roads, forest trails and well waymarked footpaths.

SHORTER VARIANT   (see Days 1 & 2)
A two-day version: *Train to Titisee;* 1 - walk from Titisee to Feldberger-hof; 2 - ascend Feldberg; walk from Feldberger-hof to Bärental (not described but there is a waymarked path) and hence to Titisee.

VILLAGES
Bärental (population 400), Titisee (4000), **Hinterzarten** (2400), **Feldberger-hof** (<100), **Muggenbrunn** (400), **Wieden** (570), Aftersteg (400), **Todtnau** (5100).

ACCOMMODATION   There is a range of hotels, varying in price and style, at each overnight stop.

CUISINE
The Black Forest is home to Germany's best cooking. Specialities include *Schwarzwalder Schinken* (smoked ham), *Schaufele* (marinated smoked pork shoulder), *Hirschragout* (venison stew), *Wildschwein* (wild boar) and *Wildentenbrust* (wild duck). The forests provide trout from the streams, various mushrooms, forest fruits and the renowned Black Forest honey. Its best known export is the *Schwarzwalder Kirschtorte*, a cake made with cherries soaked in *Kirschwasser*, the most famous of the Black Forest liqueurs.

WILDLIFE
The forest canopy shelters a profuse array of wildflowers in spring and summer and fungi in the autumn. The area is home to many butterfly species and there is a variety of birdlife including owls, woodpeckers and dippers near the many streams. The woods are also home to lizards, squirrels, foxes, deer and boar.

SPECIAL FEATURES
Titisee's crystal waters; romantic forest paths; the valley settings of Hinterzarten, Wieden and Todtnau; Feldsee, a remote glacial lake; the panoramas from Feldberg and Belchen; the Todtnauer Wasserfall.

FURTHER READING

WALKING IN THE BLACK FOREST
by Fleur & Colin Speakman, published by Cicerone Press, 1990

USEFUL ADDRESSES

SCHWARTZWALD TOURISMUSVERBAND (TOURIST OFFICE)
Postfach 1660, D-79016 Freiburg, Tel: 0761) 31317; Fax: 0761) 36021
Internet website: http://www.schwarzwald-tourist-info.de

HIKING AROUND FELDBERG - for a luggage-free hike approximating this route, contact:
Tourist-Information, D-79822 Titisee-Neustadt, Tel: 07651) 206251; Fax: 07651) 4436

SAXON SWITZERLAND

Unrivalled hiking in Germany's newest national park, through the deeply eroded sandstone plateau of the upper Elbe river valley where the fantastic rock formations make for a unique landscape.

Saxon Switzerland (Sächsische Schweiz) is the common but misleading name given to the area between Dresden and the Czech Republic's North Bohemia. It was so named after its unusual rock formations were captured in landscapes by Swiss artists in the 18th century, when Dresden was the centre of Germany's Romantic movement. Many leading artists such as Canaletto, Caspar David Friedrich and Otto Dix painted the landscapes of the Elbe Sandstone Mountains.

This landscape, unique in Europe, is anything but Swiss. The Elbe and its tributaries have deeply eroded the plateau formed from sediment deposited during the Cretaceous period when the region was part of the Cretaceous sea. Erosion has sculpted U-shaped valleys, blocks, stepped walls and isolated needles and towers. Forests cling to rock outcrops and deep-cut gorges are a sanctuary for many rare plants, now protected by the creation in 1990 of the Nationalpark Sächsische Schweiz, the newest of Germany's eleven national parks. The area provides over 1200 km of waymarked paths beckoning the walker with some of Germany's best hiking. Not surprisingly, the thousand or so freestanding rock towers are a paradise for climbers. In fact the sport of free-climbing (with no artificial aids) was born here.

Saxon Switzerland's medieval history has left its mark on this amazing landscape. Once it was a possession of Bohemia before falling under the sovereignty of the Margraves of Meissen and later the Electors of Saxony whose official seat was Hohnstein fortress at one time. Ruins of castles once the stronghold of robber barons can be found on some of the most inaccessible summits, a legacy of the region's importance as a trading route between Bohemia and Saxony.

Our five day walk is on both sides of the beautiful river Elbe and visits many of the area's most delightful villages. It takes you to all the highlights of the national park and surrounds: the famous Bastei Rocks, the viewpoints of Lilienstein and Pfaffenstein with its Barbarine rock needle, the Konigstein fortress, the Schrammsteine ridge with its many viewpoints and summits and the beautiful Polenz valley and Obere Schleuse gorge.

The massive Schrammsteine looms over the otherwise flat landscape of the Elbe river valley.

DAY ONE - KRIPPEN TO KÖNIGSTEIN (18.5 KM; 8 HRS)

Today's walking is confined to the south side of the Elbe with the town of Königstein as the ultimate objective. En route are possible ascents of the summits of Kohlbornstein, Papststein, Gohrisch and Pfaffenstein, providing panoramic views of the Elbe valley and the Königstein fortress and close-up encounters with dramatic rock formations. Our route begins at Krippen, a village lining the Krippenbach on the south bank of the Elbe.

From Krippen's S-bahn station, walk left on road parallel to the railway line for 400 m before turning right onto Friedrich Gottlob-Keller Strasse. Continue up through Krippen to a road junction and take the right fork signed to Papstdorf. Soon veer left steeply uphill into forest on a grassy path, the Koppelbergweg (waymarked with a red dot). Continue ascending on the red dot path ignoring other paths and forest roads. At a clearing with a picnic table detour left off the red dot path for 500 m to the summit of Kohlbornstein (371 m). This involves climbing wooden steps to the first sandstone formation, then walking along a narrow ridge until you reach the viewpoint at the end of the table mountain. From here take in the extensive pastoral views down to Krippen, east to Zirkelstein and north-west to Lilienstein.

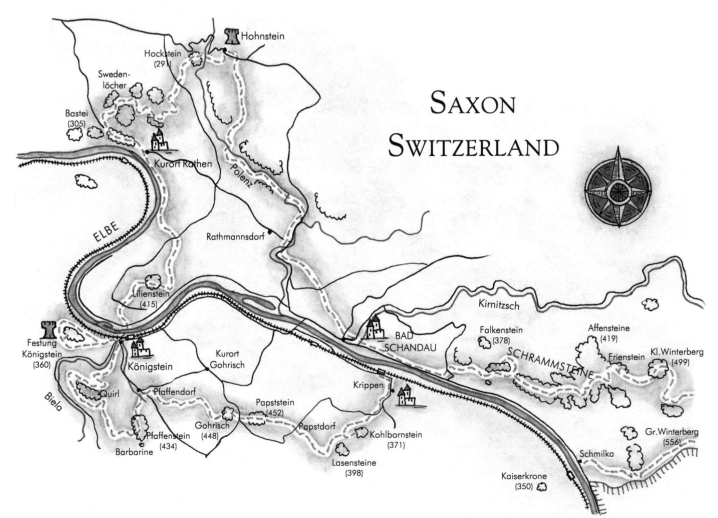

Return past the picnic table to the crosspaths and head for Papstdorf, turning left onto a track on the edge of forest and across farmland. Turn right onto a minor road and follow it through Papstdorf's outskirts. Cross the main road at a bus stop where there are many fingerboard signs and take the route signed 'Papststein and Pfaffenstein 2.5 hours' (red dot) for the ascent of Papststein (452 m). From the summit there are extensive views and an orientation table on the lookout facing Festung Königstein. There is also a gasthaus where lunch could be had. *The path descends the western side of the table mountain and crosses a road at a parking bay, continuing on the red dot path. Soon diverge right uphill on the path signed 'Aufsteig zum Gohrisch'.* The steps to Gohrisch's summit (448 m) climb through several impressive rock fissures to reach a shelter and an orientation table. Gohrisch is fascinating to explore: make the detour to Wetterfahnen-Aussicht for views over the spa village of Kurort Gohrisch and Königstein. Other detours on the plateau include the Schwedenhölle and the Falkenschlucht, an incredibly steep and tight crevice accessed by metal ladders. *Descend the western side of Gohrisch and go left at a path fork signed 'Muselweg Gohrisch 25 min'. At a junction take the level yellow stripe path to a T-junction where you turn left (yellow dot path marked 'Jagdsteig'). Skirt meadowland and continue through woodland to reach a crosspaths where you take the green stripe path straight ahead. Turn left at a minor road where you obtain superb views to Festung Königstein. Turn right at a T-junction and soon after turn left at a parking bay at Pfaffendorf. Ascend Pfaffenstein (435 m) on the Nadelohraufsteig (Eye of the Needle) steps which negotiate a narrow rock crevice.*

Pfaffenstien, an eroded table mountain inhabited in prehistoric times, is the perfect vantage point for viewing Königstein's fortress. Paths and steps on the summit allow access to numerous viewpoints and bizarre formations, notably the Barbarine, a 60 m freestanding rock pillar which is a famous landmark. Meals can be purchased at the summit gasthaus. *From*

Look out for the many rock climbers who are drawn to the area.

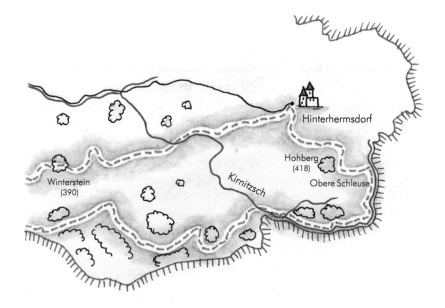

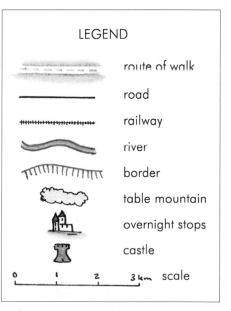

LEGEND

	route of walk
	road
	railway
	river
	border
	table mountain
	overnight stops
	castle
0 1 2 3 km	scale

Festung Königstein's fortifications (above) and (below) the view of the castle from the river.

here take the red dot path and after some steps join a broad, sandstone paved path which leads through a bronze-age wall which once protected the settlement above. Follow signs for Quirl, crossing meadow and entering woodland. Remain on the red dot path which contours below the Quirl rocks through delightful forest and presently reaches the deep Diebskeller cave. Here the path drops to reach a junction by an old milestone where you take the left downhill path signposted to Königstein. After joining a gravel path, reach a minor paved road at a hairpin bend and go left downhill. Königstein is a pleasant riverside town whose main drawcard is the nearby fortress. It has a tourist office, bank and several hotels and gasthauses.

DAY TWO - KÖNIGSTEIN TO KURORT RATHEN (14.5 KM; 6 HRS)

Following a visit to the extraordinary fortress above Königstein, today's route crosses the Elbe to climb to the viewpoint of Lilienstein and descend to the village of Kurort Rathen nestled beneath the famous Bastei rocks.

Festung Königstein more than repays the steep climb (30-40 minutes) from Königstein, the 360° perimeter views being a prime reward. Covering 9.5 hectares and with rock walls up to 40 m high, the once impregnable fortress rises majestically from the table mountain and overlooks a picturesque meander in the Elbe. Its history spans 750 years and it was first fortified in 1589 by Christian I, Elector of Saxony. Over the centuries leading to the Napoleonic period, its fortifications were repeatedly strengthened: as a result it contains late Gothic, Renaissance, Baroque and 19th century buildings. The remarkable 16th century housed well, dug over six years, is 152 m deep. Tours in English are available and there are several museums.

Back at Königstein, catch the ferry across the Elbe, turn right and quickly left, ascending a blue stripe waymarked path signed to Lilienstein. You are now on the E3, a European long distance trail. After a steep climb ignoring left forks, turn left onto a minor road and very soon turn right onto a track crossing fields to enter national park. Lilienstein (415 m) towers above its forest surrounds: as you approach, look up for rock climbers on its sheerest walls. Metal ladders assist the steep climb to the summit plateau where there is a gasthaus and an obelisk attesting that Lilienstein was hiked in 1708 (before ladders!) by Augustus the Strong, most famous of Saxony's Electors. Lilienstein provides perhaps Saxon Switzerland's most extensive panoramas from its three main viewpoints. The view from the Westhorn, an outcrop connected to the plateau by bridge, is toward the Bastei and beyond to Pirna and Dresden. The Königsteiner Aussicht takes in the south of the Elbe: not only the fortress but all of the previous day's route and, more distantly, the Erzgebirge mountains. From the Carolabastei the view is up river to Bad Schandau and the Schrammsteine and beyond the border into Bohemia. *Descend the other side of Lilienstein still on the blue stripe path which turns N and passes a pathside monument, a Jewish memorial. The path re-enters forest, swinging NW and crossing a minor road before descending a small gorge to reach the bank of the Elbe and follow the river to Kurort Rathen.* This small health resort sitting prettily on the Elbe at the foot of the Bastei is a much frequented spot and is famous for the nearby Felsenbühne open-air theatre.

The table mountain of Lilienstein overlooks a meander in the Elbe.

DAY THREE - KURORT RATHEN TO BAD SCHANDAU (18 KM; 7 HRS)

Today's route takes you over the strangely sculpted Bastei Rocks and the Hockstein cliff above the river Polenz to the perched village of Hohnstein and then south once more to the Elbeside town of Bad Schandau.

From Kurort Rathen's main street, it is a steep 30 minute walk to the famous Bastei on the blue stripe waymarked path. You pass the Felsenburg Neurathen, ruins of a 13th century fortress secreted among the natural rock formations. The path now crosses the Basteibrücke, a 76 m bridge built in 1851 to span the Mardertelle gorge. Detour right to the Ferdinandstein for the best view of this sandstone bridge with the Steinschleuder rock jutting out behind. The Bastei, some 190 m above the Elbe, provides stunning views in all directions over river and forest.

The descent from the Bastei (blue stripe path) is through the romantic Schwedenlöcher Gorge, used as a hiding place during the Great Northern War in 1709, to the Amselgrund. Reaching a T-junction, detour left briefly to visit the national park information centre and the Amselfall which, curiously, flows only on payment to the kiosk operator. *Backtrack downstream and continue to the pretty Amselsee, a tiny dam on which hired boats can be rowed. Take the green stripe path, a track which winds up through dense forest. Almost 1 km after crossing a road, turn right at a path junction. Soon cross the Teufelsbrucke (Devil's Bridge) built in 1821 to the Hockstein summit and view-*

109

The view from the Basteibrücke.

*Well-preserved buildings feature
in the old quarter of Hohnstein.*

point. The Hockstein (291 m), once the site of a medieval castle, towers over the Polenz river valley giving excellent views across to the village of Hohnstein. *Descend to the valley floor through the Wolfsschlucht (Wolf's Ravine) on metal stairs which corkscrew down through a rock chasm. Turn right onto the valley road (blue stripe) and at a gasthaus turn left over the Polenz. The path ascends the gorge of a small tributary, climbing up past the ruins of the Bärengarten, built in 1609 and through which the stream was diverted, to arrive at the town's outskirts.* Picturesque Hohnstein (*High Stone*) adjoins the national park and clusters beneath a 14th century fortress which now houses a Youth Hostel, museum, lookout tower and cafe-restaurant.

From Hohnstein, follow the road signed to Brand (blue stripe) to the edge of the national park and fork right on the red stripe path signed to Waltersdorfer Mühle. Enter forest and descend a narrow gully lined with lichen-covered rock formations to reach the river Polenz. On a broad track follow the river downstream passing the old mill on the opposite bank before crossing over on a 1898 bridge. Continue downstream then recross the river on a wooden bridge, continuing along the other bank. Turn right onto the main road (blue stripe route) and follow it for 1 km along the Lachsbach. After several bends leave the road left on the red dot path for Rathmannsdorf, cross a road and continue into Bad Schandau. Overlooked by the massive Schrammsteine crags, Bad Schandau lines the Elbe's right bank at its confluence with the Kirnitzsch. It partitions the national park and is the area's chief resort, spa and hiking base. On the Kirnitzschtalbahn, one of only two extant rural tramlines in Germany, you can follow the Kirnitzsch 8 km upstream. Panoramic views can be had by taking the *Personenaufzug*, a quaint iron lift on the town's eastern outskirts.

DAY FOUR - BAD SCHANDAU TO HINTERHERMSDORF (23 KM; 9 HRS)

Today's traverse of the Schrammsteine plateau and several other summits is quite demanding but the scenery is breathtaking for the sandstone outcrops are at their most savage and bizarre in this section of the park. Take lunch supplies and plenty of water.

From Bad Schandau, follow the yellow stripe route along the Elbeside road and then up left to meet the climbing Ostrau road. Soon turn right off road to enter national park. In 700 m you join the blue stripe path through the Schrammtor pass. You are now face to face with the savage beauty of the Schrammsteine massif, a continuous ridge of bizarre rock formations which appear impenetrable from below. *A steep climb on the Jagersteig metal ladders will see you to the ridge top.* Detour left (green dot path) for the spectacular panorama from the Schrammsteine Aussicht (417 m): the precipitous needle of the Vorderer Torstein, a magnet for fearless climbers, is framed by the Elbe valley. *Return to follow the ridge top Gratweg path (blue stripe) which offers a succession of views before reaching a junction where you should detour left for 10 minutes to Carolafelsen for a magnificent view of the Falkenstein and Lilienstein beyond. Back on the ridgepath, turn left onto an unwaymarked path for Frienstein. Soon fork right (green stripe path); Frienstein is a short but dramatic detour on a narrow path around the base of large stone blocks.* Frienstein has views, a cave and the scant remains of a castle, one of many built by robber barons.

Backtrack to the green stripe path which contours Kleiner Winterberg where a rock platform provides views and a possible location for lunch. Follow the circuitous red stripe path for Winterstein (390 m). The summit ascent involves a 10 minute detour negotiating metal ladders and hand rails. It is difficult to imagine how the medieval castle which once crowned the summit could have been built. A few ruins remain and the views are superb. *Return to the red stripe path which now descends to meet a gravel track. Follow this right to soon reach the Zeughausstrasse (an old trade road) which you follow right to reach the few buildings and gasthof at Zeughaus. Just before the last building, turn left uphill and soon fork right uphill on a broad track (blue stripe, signed to Hinterhermsdorf) through the Thorwald. The road then zigzags downhill, crossing the Kirnitzsch at the Thorwalder Brücke. Turn right and follow the pretty river upstream before forking left uphill at the next road junction. Follow this and the Dorfbachweg for 2.5 km to reach Hinterhermsdorf.* Set above lush, rolling farmland, Hinterhermsdorf is a sleepy border village with a museum, tourist office and several hotels. It also has a bus connection to Bad Schandau.

Day Five - Hinterhermsdorf to Schmilka (21 km; 7.5 hrs)

Today's journey completes the near-circular traverse of the Nationalpark Hintere Sächsische Schweiz along the Czech border. A highlight is the boat ride on the Obere Schleuse and subsequent walk beside the Kirnitzsch's upper reaches. It is again remote so carry lunch provisions and water.

The formations of Schrammsteine and freestanding Falkenstein, with Lilienstein and Königstein visible in the background.

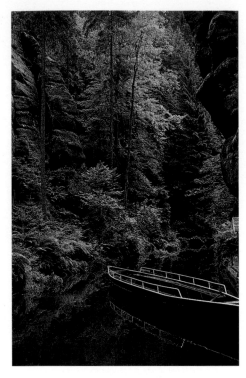

*Lush vegetation fills the gorge
at Obere Schleuse.*

Leave Hinterhermsdorf south on Bruchenstrasse, turning left onto a gravel road just before the park entrance (blue stripe route signed to Obere Schleuse). Descend gently through forest, at one point shortcutting the road on a path, to descend to the boat station. A leisurely guided boat ride through the beautiful, fern-lined waters of the gorge takes 30 minutes; alternatively, the path follows above the gorge. Disembark to rejoin the blue stripe path climbing above the Kirnitzsch. Presently you encounter the enclosed Wolfschlucht chasm; you'll have to bend low to get through. Follow the blue stripe path along the river valley to a bridge: cross the river and follow the green stripe path signed to Hickelhöhle. Climb on a gravel track and at a curve fork right through woods. Contour the Raumberg and reach Altarstein where a large stone bears a carved inscription. At a path junction fork left (green stripe) to ascend and descend over a narrow pass to Hickelhöhle, an impressive rock overhang offering a good lunch spot.

Take the red stripe path which soon joins the gravel Zeughaus road and follow this NW along the forested Zshand for 2 km. Turn left (SW) onto a green dot path which makes a descent and steep ascent through the Richterschlüchte. This is a place to savour: at the gorge's narrowest point, you are closely surrounded by sheer rock walls. Once out of the gorge the path hairpins before reaching a junction where you take the blue stripe path. This follows the Czech border generally SW. At one point you can detour right uphill to Grosser Winterberg, the highest point in the national park (556 m, gasthaus). Otherwise, descend on the hairpin mountain road (red dot path), eventually leaving the road left to take the red dot forest path steeply down to Schmilka. The little Elbeside village of Schmilka, almost on the Czech border, has a bahnhof across the river and limited accommodation. The return to Krippen is a pretty 7 km riverside walk on the south bank or take the S-bahn to the next stop.

NOTES ON SAXON SWITZERLAND

TYPE OF WALK   Near circular

LENGTH OF WALK   95 kilometres (59 miles); 5 days

DIFFICULTY   A medium grade walk with one long day and steep sections

START & FINISH   Krippen and Schmilka, neighbouring villages on the upper Elbe river

PUBLIC TRANSPORT
From Dresden Hauptbahnhof, take the suburban S-bahn #1 to Krippen (1 hour) and return from Schona to Dresden the same way (the ferry is a picturesque but slower alternative).

LUGGAGE   You can store excess luggage at Dresden Hauptbahnhof.

CLIMATE
Central European, with warm summers and winter snow. Best walking is from late May to October.

MAP
Kompass Wander- und Radtourenkarte 1028 1:50,000 *Sächsische Schweiz*

PATH
The entire route is on backroads and waymarked footpaths.

SHORTER VARIANT (see Days 2, 3 & 4)
Two-day version: *S-bahn from Dresden to Königstein*; 1- visit Festung; walk from Königstein to Kurort Rathen then side trip to Bastei; 2 - *S-bahn to Bad Schandau*; return walk to Schrammsteine; *catch S-bahn*.

VILLAGES
Krippen (population approx. 250), **Königstein** (2900), **Kurort Rathen** (500), Hohnstein (4050), **Bad Schandau** (3050), **Hinterhermsdorf** (800), Schmilka (300).

ACCOMMODATION
The area is well supplied with reasonably priced hotels, private rooms and Youth Hostels.

CUISINE
Regional Saxon specialities include *Kartoffelsuppe* (hearty potato soup), *Zwiebelfleisch* (a casserole made with onions) and *Geschmorte Grillhaxe vom Schwein* (roasted knuckle of pork). *Quarkkeulchen* are delicious pancakes made with potatoes and cheese. Herbal liqueur–*Kräutlikör*–is made locally.

WILDLIFE
The National Park's forests shelter many rare plants including the silver fir, thorny shield fern, water buttercup, yellow violet, forest barley, and marsh ledum. Rare or endangered animals include the lynx, otter (along the Kirnitzsch), water shrew, peregrine falcon, kingfisher and black woodpecker. Birds of prey are often to be seen from the high viewpoints.

SPECIAL FEATURES
The Lilienstein and Pfaffenstein summit with its Barbarine rock needle; Königstein's massive fortress; the Bastei Rocks and sandstone bridge; the Obere Schleuse and the Kirnitzsch river valley; the bizarre rock forms and viewpoints of the Schrammsteine; the forested and clifflined Elbe river valley.

FURTHER READING

HIGHLIGHTS OF SAXON SWITZERLAND
A booklet published in various languges by Edition Lipp, Germany, 1993

USEFUL ADDRESSES

TOURISMUSVERBAND SÄCHSISCHE SCHWEIZ
Am Bahnhof 6, 01814 Bad Schandau, Ph: 035022) 49530; Fax: 035022) 49533

NATIONALPARK SÄCHSISCHE SCHWEIZ
Head Office, Schandauer Strasse 34 01824 Königstein, Ph: 035021) 68229

Heart of Scotland

A gentle introduction to the wild grandeur of the Scottish Highlands on a delightful circular walk which takes in charming villages, pristine lochs and rivers, heather-clad hills and remote glens.

The Highlands of Scotland are among Europe's least populated regions and are often thought of as remnant wilderness. Yet this is a man-made wilderness: little remains of the once vast tracts of primaeval Caledonian forest. The quintessential highland landscape of denuded, heather-clad hills and moorland is the result of deforestation and the 19th century clearances in which tenant farmers and their crops were replaced by grazing sheep or the land turned over to deer and grouse hunting. This sometimes forbidding landscape, set against a backdrop of sparkling lochs and long river glens, gives the Highlands its unique character.

The geological fault line known as the Highland Line runs from coast to coast and marks the boundary between the rolling farmland of the central Lowlands and the mountainous terrain of the Highlands to the north. Our walk is in the north-west of Perthshire, a county partitioned by the Highland Line. Dunkeld, our starting point, straddles the Line and was long a meeting place for highland and lowland cultures. In fact it was proclaimed Scotland's original ecclesiastical capital by its first king, Kenneth MacAlpin, in 850. Perthshire is truly Scotland in miniature and our route passes through its diverse landscapes: the rich sweep of Strath Tay, the bleakness of Glen Garry and Glenmore, the scenic beauty of Lochs Rannoch and Tay and the many burns which tumble through thick forest. You will also visit some of Perthshire's loveliest villages where you can revel in traditional hospitality.

This walk is not for intrepid mountaineers or obsessive 'peak baggers'. It has been planned to minimise the dangers and rigours often associated with highland walking and the only mountain ascent is an optional diversion. Nevertheless, you must pay due regard to the notoriously changeable climate and be adequately equipped, especially if walking out of season. Scottish land is privately owned–there are no National Parks–and maps do not show rights of way as they do in England. Traditionally, there is a 'freedom to roam' over unfenced and uncultivated land though restrictions apply during hunting seasons. You will often be walking on disused tracks and you will likely have these to yourself. Savour the solitude!

Duinish bothy, frequented only by grazing sheep, stands in the remote Glen Garry.

115

DAY ONE - DUNKELD TO BALLINLUIG (18.5 KM; 5.5 HRS)

After exploring Dunkeld, today's journey is a delightful and undemanding ramble through the forests of the Atholl Estate above Dunkeld, taking in several small lochs and following high above Strath Tay towards Pitlochry. One of Scotland's prettiest towns with its wealth of restored, whitewashed buildings, Dunkeld nestles on the left bank of the river Tay surrounded by thickly wooded hills. Dunkeld's majestic cathedral, partly in ruins, is idyllically sited on tree-studded lawns which slope down to the Tay. Our journey begins on the north side of Thomas Telford's 1809 seven-arched bridge over the Tay. *After buying lunch provisions, turn right uphill into Brae St, looking back to admire the unfolding views of the cathedral and town. Turn left at the edge of Craig Wood, following the Fungarth Walk (waymarked with a 'yellow man' icon) up Fungarth Hill past juniper trees on the lower slopes. Turn left onto a minor road to the Loch of Lowes Wildlife Centre. The nature reserve here is managed by the Scottish Wildlife Trust. Visit the observation hide where,* during breeding season, you can view the famous pair of resident ospreys at their eyrie. Otters have also been seen on the loch.

Continue on road and turn left onto the A923. After 700 m, climb steps on the right through forest, initially above the road and skirting Crieff Hill. Go right onto a broad track into Atholl Estates woods following yellow waymarks to The Glack. The track heads N for Mill Dam, leaving forest for moorland after bridging the Birkenburn. Quintessential Scottish views of heather-clad hills and crags soon open up. Look for fallow deer grazing in woodland clearings or on moorland and for wildfowl at Mill Dam. *From the dam bear NW on the track, soon leaving the yellow waymarks. The scenery is superb as you pass Rotmell and Dowally Lochs, either making a pleasant lunch spot. Soon reach Raor Lodge, now a farmhouse, where you bear right and then left over a stone bridge above a cascading burn. The grassy path offers extensive views over beautiful Strath Tay and of distant Pitlochry ahead. Continue N beneath rocky crags until the track cuts back sharply; here press ahead on a narrow footpath. Contour up to a large tree and then descend gently towards a farmhouse where you climb a stile and skirt a field to pick up the farm track down to a minor road. Here turn right for a pleasant road walk of some 4 km to reach Ballinluig.*

From Ballinluig there are frequent afternoon buses for Pitlochry: you could walk the 10 or so km on minor roads but that would leave no time to explore Pitlochry. This bustling town, spread along the eastern shore of the river Tummel, has good train and bus connections, a theatre and plenty of accommodation. As well as shops full of woollens, there are two nearby distilleries to be sampled. Across the river you can observe salmon and trout ascending the fish ladder, part of the Loch Faskally dam.

The whitewashed buildings of Dunkeld cluster around the ancient Cathedral.

HEART OF SCOTLAND

LEGEND

route of walk

bus link

road

railway

river; waterfall

mountain peak

overnight stop

castle; feature

scale

*Blair Castle, the seat of
the Dukedom of Atholl.*

*The peat-stained waters of the
Allt Coire Easan in Glen Garry.*

DAY TWO - PITLOCHRY TO BLAIR ATHOLL (13 KM; 4 HRS)

Today's is an easy half-day walk initially following the line of an ancient highway used for over a thousand years, then descending to the historic Pass of Killiecrankie before following the river Garry into Blair Atholl.

From the main street, turn uphill onto Larchwood Rd towards the hamlet of Moulin, following orange and purple waymarks. Winding uphill through forest, you soon reach the Cuilc, formerly a marl pit and now an attractive pond with resident waterfowl. Continue on through rolling pastureland. At a T-junction, where you might admire the view over Pitlochry, you can make a short detour right to see the Dane's Stone (an isolated standing stone) in a field. Another field harbours a 14th century ruin, Caisteal Dubh (Black Castle). Back at the junction, continue W on the Old North Road along which journeyed King Robert the Bruce in 1306, Mary, Queen of Scots in 1564 and General Mackay and his troops in 1689. Through a gate, the road becomes a track and leads uphill through Pitlochry golf course to plantation forest. In the forest you can detour right for the short, steep ascent of Craigower Hill (Goat's Crag), owned by the National Trust for Scotland (NTS). From its 400 m summit are excellent views N through Glen Garry to the Drumochter mountains and W along Loch Tummel as far as the Paps of Glencoe. The view S is along Strath Tay to Loch Faskally. *Back on the main track, walk high above the main road with views down to the Pass of Killiecrankie from forest clearings. After some 3 km you descend steps to walk under the A9 and emerge right onto General Wade's Military Rd, one of many built to counter Highland uprisings.*

Soon reach the Pass of Killiecrankie NTS Visitor's Centre. In 1689 this beautiful tree-lined gorge of the river Garry was the scene of the first of the Jacobite rebellions when General Mackay's government troops were routed by the forces of Viscount 'Bonnie' Dundee who died in battle. Descend to view Soldier's Leap, a 4.5 m-wide chasm over which a fleeing soldier is said to have jumped. *Now cut back up to the road, pass the quaint Killiecrankie school and turn left onto a minor road shortly after the Post Office. Crossing the bridge over the Garry, there are good views down the gorge. Fork right following the river upstream and take the 'private road' right under the A9, continuing by the riverside to a footbridge across the Garry.* Blair Atholl sits serenely at the confluence of the Garry and the Tilt. Whitewashed, turreted Blair Castle, one of Scotland's most popular attractions, is nearby. Its tower dates from 1269 but it is mostly 18th century. The castle was the last in Britain to be besieged (by Jacobites in 1746) and today the Duke is the only British subject permitted to maintain a private army, the Atholl Highlanders.

DAY THREE - DALNASPIDAL TO KINLOCH RANNOCH (20 KM; 6.5 HRS)

Civilisation is left far behind on today's walk by the austere and remote Loch Garry and through beautiful moorland to the shores of Loch Rannoch. *After buying lunch provisions, catch a bus to Calvine where you can catch the 4-seater postbus (book in advance) along Glen Garry to Dalnaspidal Lodge, now a farm just south of the A9. The signed public right of way to Kinloch Rannoch leaves to the right of a stone outbuilding through paddocks. The farm track crosses* bridges to reach the head of Loch Garry and leads along its left bank beneath Meallan Buidhe. It ends just below falls on Allt Coire Easan near the loch's southern shore. Ford this allt or stream carefully and look for tyre marks in the boggy ground, the only sign of the continuing path beneath the slopes of Meall Doire. After 1.3 km you reach the banks of Allt Shallainn: walk upstream (a footpad should emerge) for 250 m to cross on a wooden bridge and pick up a track which fords a minor stream several times and heads SE uphill. Reach the lonely Duinish *bothy* (a hut for farmhands) at a fork in picturesque surroundings, a good place for a late lunch in the company of grazing sheep.

The track now crosses Allt na Duinish and contours uphill between Gualann Sheileach and Creag a' Mhadaidh, providing distant views of Schiehallion. The path levels and then descends to a junction near forest where you take the left fork, waymarked with a yellow arrow. Ahead are the waters of Loch Rannoch. Ignoring a track right, skirt the forest then loop S downhill. The track fords the Annat Burn; find a crossing place upstream if the burn is in spate. Pass ruins and a pretty, willowed grove then go through a gate and between drystone walls. After several more gates, walk through Annat farm to the lochside road where you turn left for Kinloch Rannoch. In several places you can scramble down to the water's edge to view the loch but you can't really avoid the road walk. On reaching the time-share development just out of the village, you can pick up another public footpath to Kinloch Rannoch via a spectacular cascade on the Allt Mór. Kinloch Rannoch is an attractive, isolated village on the river Tummel and on the ancient 'Road to the Isles'. There is a choice of hotels and B&Bs; an infrequent bus service runs to Pitlochry.

DAY FOUR - KINLOCH RANNOCH TO FORTINGALL (16.5 KM; 5 HRS)

This is a wild day's walk to exquisite Fortingall village through beautiful Glenmore on lonely tracks and over moorland with the option of an energetic scramble up Schiehallion's scree for one of Scotland's best panoramas.

After purchasing lunch supplies, leave Kinloch Rannoch by the unnumbered road SE across the bridge. Cross Innerhadden Burn and, some 3 km from the village, Tempar Burn. At a road curve, climb a stile on the right where a sign warns against walking during deer stalking season (21 Sep to 21 Oct); there are no waymarks on this route which is through private estates. Initially faint, the path leads up by the burn and through several gates before beginning to contour around Schiehallion's lower slopes. There are lovely views back to Dunalastair Water. The track steepens and presently you reach a tiny bothy built into a hillside, serving as an emergency shelter. Here the track ends and a very narrow footpad or sheeptrack continues through the heather. The pad, indistinct and boggy, leads high above the silvery thread of Glenmore Burn. When it disappears completely continue through heather in the same direction and avoid losing height.

Once the Glenmore Bothy is in sight, find a conspicuous place to leave excess gear if you wish to detour to climb Schiehallion. The pathless 600 m ascent is steep and strenuous (allow 3 hours up and back), initially through heather below the scree line and then a scramble over boulders and scree until the rocky summit (1083 m) is gained. Schiehallion–the Fairy Hill of the Caledonians–is a

Schiehallion's distinctive conical form is a landmark for some distance around.

119

deservedly popular climb and you will likely share the summit with arrivals on the official route from Braes of Foss. On a clear day, the Highland views are magnificent: W to Loch Rannoch and beyond to bleak Rannoch Moor and distant, snowcapped Ben Nevis; N to Ben Macdhui and the Cairngorms; E over Strath Tummel and S over Glenmore. Schiehallion's almost perfect conical shape enabled an early attempt by the Astronomer Royal in 1774 to calculate the earth's density by measuring the mountain's gravitational attraction on a pendulum hung nearby.

Return to your pack and make your way down to Glenmore Burn just before its confluence with Allt Creag a' Mhadaidh. Cross the burn on stepping stones, pass ruined shielings and soon reach and cross the allt on stepping stones. Try to find the faint path up to Glenmore bothy and pick up a track above the bothy and to its right. This track ascends for some 2 km to the shoulder of Meall Crumach before commencing a long and gradual descent. Traversing this lonely road, it is hard to believe that in 1750, after it was built and before the highland clearances, there were 26 independent settlements or villages dotted around these slopes surrounding Fortingall. As you near Fortingall, superb views open up over the mouth of Glen Lyon to Loch Tay. *Zigzag steeply downhill, then walk between farm buildings to reach the sealed road where you turn left into Fortingall.* Nestled below forested hills by the River Lyon, tiny Fortingall is one of Scotland's most charming villages. Amazingly for its size, it has two claims to fame: as the legendary birthplace of Pontius Pilate and for the yew tree growing in its churchyard, which at over 3000 years old is considered to be Europe's oldest living vegetation. Fortingall has no shop but has a hotel and B&B and an infrequent bus connection to Aberfeldy.

Fortingall village boasts thatched cottages covered with espaliered roses.

DAY FIVE - FORTINGALL TO ABERFELDY (26.5 KM; 8 HRS)

Today's varied walk takes you over Drummond Hill and down to pretty Kenmore, along Loch Tay to the Falls of Acharn and above Strath Tay to Aberfeldy. Buses from Acharn to Aberfeldy allow the walk to be shortened.

Leave Fortingall on the road E and just after the left turn-off to Balnacraig farm, take a footpath right through a gate to reach the suspension footbridge over the languid River Lyon. Through Duneaves farm turn left onto a minor road and, near the river, cut sharply back right up to Kinnighallen farm, picking up the grassy track behind the farmhouse. Head left and through a gate to enter Drummond Hill, Scotland's oldest managed forest. Take the track left uphill, ignoring turn-offs, and turn sharp right at crosspaths onto a track marked with blue and red stripes on a post. Follow the blue waymarks: the path ascends Drummond Hill SW and then swings NE. Make a short detour right to Black Rock lookout for a most beautiful view over Kenmore. *Continue downhill on the blue path to the main forest gate and take a footpath right downhill to turn right onto road and cross the 1774 bridge over the Tay and into Kenmore.* Little changed since Victorian times, the heritage village of Kenmore has an attractive square flanked by mid-18th century whitewashed cottages and its 1572 hotel (reputedly Scotland's oldest) where Robert Burns penned a poem on a wall. The magnificent archway dominating the short main street is all that remains of Balloch Castle which predated Taymouth Castle.

Drummond Hill offers wonderful views of Kenmore and Loch Tay.

Leave Kenmore on the A827 and soon take the lochside road for Acharn. In 400 m you reach the Crannog Centre, a fascinating archeological reconstruction of an Iron Age defensive crannog dwelling built above the water. Allow an hour for the guided tour. *Cross Acharn Burn into the hamlet of Acharn and take the road left which becomes a track and climbs steeply.* Some 700 m on, detour left to the Hermit's Cave, a long chamber built into the rock leading to a lookout over an impressive waterfall. Back on the track, take the signed path left for the wooden bridge and viewing platform for the upper cascades. *Over the bridge you can descend to Acharn on a woodland path east of the burn and catch a bus to Aberfeldy (check times beforehand).*

Otherwise, take the path right uphill soon joining a track which curves up left towards plantation. Pass right of a small tumulus with views over Loch Tay. Cross Remony Burn and take level farm tracks NE, gaining superb views of the River Tay, until you reach the surfaced road to Glen Quaich. Turn right and soon gain views down to Taymouth Castle. At Tombuie Cottage, climb a fence to take a path left downhill. This heads for forest and forks right soon after to reach 'the Tower'. Enter a field (there is a sign warning of wild boars) and it's level walking for some 1.5 km until the path reaches forest. At a junction turn right uphill. The track zigzags beneath power lines, enters more forest and then forks after 700 m. Take the left fork, pass under more power lines and continue NE. Go left at a T-junction on a track which soon loops E at Dunskiag farm. Follow this farm road for 1.75 km to reach the A826 on the outskirts of Aberfeldy.

Sheep, lochs and looming clouds are elemental in Highland landscapes.

Aberfeldy marks the exact centre of Scotland. The Victorian town is blessed with plentiful accommodation, shops, a distillery and tourist office. In the centre is a restored 1825 watermill and, nearby, the fine 1733 Wade's Bridge spans the Tay. This is overlooked on the south bank by the Black Watch Memorial erected in 1887 to commemorate the raising of the famous Highland regiment. A delightful circular nature trail leads from the town, up the Moness Burn to the Moness Falls where Burns was inspired to write his famous poem 'The Birks O'Aberfeldy'.

DAY SIX - ABERFELDY TO DUNKELD (25.5 KM; 7.5 HRS)

The first part of the return to Dunkeld involves road walking so you might prefer to catch a bus; buses run via Grandtully and Ballinluig and a postbus runs via Amulree. *If walking, take lunch provisions. Walk SW along the A826 for 6.5 km, turning left onto a forest track just past Loch na Craige. Alternatively, the intrepid hiker can avoid much of the road by heather-bashing from the top falls of Moness, using power lines for guidance. The forest track takes you between Loch Kennard and Creag a' Mhadaidh and you eventually leave forest to follow the beautiful Ballinloan Burn downstream. Bridge the burn before it meets the River Braan and follow an old military road, now a farm lane. The final few km to Birnam is by way of the lovely, waymarked Hermitage walk where the Braan's cascades can be viewed from Ossian's Hall, an extraordinary folly managed by the NTS. Dunkeld is just over the Tay bridge from Birnam.*

NOTES ON HEART OF SCOTLAND

TYPE OF WALK	Circular, with two bus links
LENGTH OF WALK	120 kilometres (74.5 miles); six days
DIFFICULTY	An easy-moderate grade walk with two long days which can be shortened
START & FINISH	Dunkeld, a picturesque cathedral town astride the river Tay

PUBLIC TRANSPORT
Train (Inverness line) from Edinburgh or Glasgow to Dunkeld (also stops at Pitlochry and Blair Atholl). A useful booklet of local transport is available from Perth Tourist Office. Book postbus for Day 3.

LUGGAGE
Arrange to store excess luggage at your first night's accommodation.

CLIMATE
This walk should be attempted between May and September. Scotland's weather is highly variable and you should be prepared for rain and cold even in summer. May and June are generally the driest months; midges can be a summer irritation after mid-June.

MAP
Ordnance Survey Landranger series 1: 50,000 #42 *Glen Garry & Loch Rannoch area*, #43 *Braemar to Blair Atholl* and #52 *Pitlochry to Crieff*

PATH
The route is on local right-of-way paths (some waymarked), forest tracks and minor roads.

SHORTER VARIANT (see Days 4 & 5)
A two-day version: *Bus from Pitlochry to Kinloch Rannoch;* 1 - walk from Kinloch Rannoch to Fortingall; 2 - walk from Fortingall to Aberfeldy; *bus to Pitlochry via Ballinluig.*

VILLAGES
Dunkeld (population 1050), Ballinluig (250), **Pitlochry** (2450), **Blair Atholl** (app.250), **Kinloch Rannoch** (app.250), **Fortingall** (app.120), Kenmore (app.240), Acharn (app.80), **Aberfeldy** (1950).

ACCOMMODATION
This ranges from expensive country hotels to simple guesthouse and bed-&-breakfast rooms. Choices are limited in Kinloch Rannoch and Fortingall.

CUISINE
The district's most famous dish is *atholl brose*, a sweet concoction of cream, oatmeal and whisky. It also produces delicious berries, such as raspberries and strawberries. Menus also feature general Scottish fare, including salmon, trout and venison, as well as the traditional *haggis*, a rich dish of sheep's offal.

WILDLIFE
Roe deer are a frequent sight on the hills; less common but increasing are the numbers of red squirrels, wild cats and otters. Look out for grouse, pheasant and ptarmigan, as well as ospreys at Loch of Lowes. Note that October is hunting season and dangerous for walkers.

SPECIAL FEATURES
Dunkeld Cathedral; the historic Pass of Killiecrankie and Blair Castle; Lochs Garry, Rannoch and Tay; views from Schiehallion; Fortingall village; the Birks of Aberfeldy and the Hermitage on the river Braan.

FURTHER READING

THE NATURE OF SCOTLAND
edited by Magnus Magnusson & Graham White, published by Canongate Books, UK, 1997

USEFUL ADDRESSES

PERTHSHIRE TOURIST BOARD
Lower City Mills, West Mill St, Perth, PH1 5QP Scotland
Tel: 01738) 627958 Fax: 01738) 630416 Email: perthtouristb@perthshire.co.uk

INTERNET SITE   http://www.perthshire.co.uk

THE LAKE DISTRICT

An exhilarating circuit in the heart of England's magical Lake District, encompassing rugged fells and sparkling mountain tarns, as well as picturesque valley lakes and quaint villages.

The Lake District—or more simply, the Lakes, as the locals know it—is a pocket of wonderfully craggy country in Cumbria in England's northwest, boasting enough excellent walking to fill several lifetimes. Thousands of years of glacial activity scoured out the many long valleys radiating from the central massif of volcanic rocks. A number of these are filled with the glacial lakes which give the region its name. Few roads cross the higher ground so it remains a wild place where those on foot can find some peace.

For centuries, this remote and inaccessible area was disputed border country. The Romans established themselves here for the purpose of defence. Following the demise of their empire, the native Celts established a kingdom, fending off attacks from the Angles successfully. The Norsemen, arriving by boat, were more successful. Words such as *mere* (lake), *force* (waterfall), *fell* (mountain), *tarn* (mountain pool) and *thwaite* (a clearing in a forest) come from the period when Norse settlers cleared and farmed much of the district. For centuries, the Scots and the English both laid claim to Cumbria, and it was not until raids from the north ceased that the region enjoyed a degree of agricultural prosperity. Farming is still a serious activity in the Lakes, and the patchwork of green fields enclosed by drystone walls is a delightful contrast juxtaposed against the lowering mountains.

By the late 16th century, the mineral wealth of the fells was realised. Mining for copper, graphite and iron ore employed a growing population and brought increased wealth to the Lake District. The natural beauty of the area was largely overlooked until it found an advocate in the poet William Wordsworth who led the Romantic movement which dramatically changed attitudes to wilderness. The enthusiasm of Wordsworth, a native of Cumbria, drew other writers to the Lakes and virtually initiated tourism to the region. The Lakes have also been home to John Ruskin, the great Victorian writer who pioneered conservationism, and to author Beatrix Potter who farmed land near Hawkshead.

Walking is almost a religion in the Lakes and this route will take you to many of the most revered sites. As the walk is circular, you could pick up

Evening light accentuates the colours on the path from Grasmere to Easedale Tarn.

the trail from any point such as Keswick or Grasmere or Coniston, all accessible by bus. We suggest that you skirt around to the south west and start your journey into the Lake District with a short trip by steam train on the scenic Ravenglass and Eskdale Railway. The path leads from Eskdale over a dramatic mountain pass to verdant Borrowdale, along the shores of the beautiful Derwent Water, and across remote fell country to the famous village of Grasmere. From here, it passes glittering tarns to the dramatic Langdale and thence to Coniston on the shore of another of the larger lakes. The final leg back to Eskdale takes you past the impressive remains of a Roman fort.

The weather in the Lakes can, and often does, turn nasty and climbing the fells on such occasions can be dangerous for the inexperienced. Our route restricts itself mainly to mountain passes and valleys where good walking is to be had even in poor weather. If you have ample time, there are plenty of opportunities to scale a few peaks (or *pikes* as they are known hereabouts) such as Coniston Old Man, Great Gable, or Scafell Pike. If the weather is really horrible, you can shorten the route by catching various local buses. No matter what the weather, time spent in the Lake District is time rewarded.

DAY ONE - ESKDALE GREEN TO SEATHWAITE FARM (19 KM; 7 HRS)

Today's journey is demanding, so it would be wise to start early. The route takes you over the Screes, following high above wild Wastwater and down to the isolated village of Wasdale Head, the destination for lunch. From Wasdale the way is up over Styhead, an exhilarating pass surrounded by England's grandest mountains, before a final descent to Seathwaite Farm. Take extra food supplies with you as a precaution.

Leave the village of Eskdale Green by the lane heading NE, passing the Outward Bound school. Veer left at the fork then continue across a road and a bridge over the River Mite. The path ascends on a stony track, crosses several forest roads and heads straight on. Once you leave the forest, turn right, following a wall and climbing once more. This ground can be boggy and the path indistinct. Climb the path up Whin Rigg and follow it along the top of the Screes.

From here you have a wonderful view of Wastwater, some 518 m below. This lake was carved out by a glacier at the end of the Ice Age and is 79 m deep. The *screes* or cliffs are not stable and rock falls sometimes occur, so don't walk too close to the edge. Looking west towards the coast, you may be able to see the sandstone sea plain, which gives way to the granite valleys at the base of the volcanic Cumbrian mountains. *Once you reach the summit of Illgill Head, the path descends and, at a junction of paths, you turn left.* The path you have joined is known as the Burnmoor Corpse Road, as it was once the route taken by the inhabitants of Wasdale Head to bury their dead in the nearest consecrated ground, at Boot. *Veer to the right of a small wood and continue north. Just past the end of the lake, cross a track and then cross by bridge over a gill (or stream) and over the larger Lingmell Beck. Turn right onto a road which takes you to Wasdale Head. This small village, nestled*

A wintry view of Sty Head Tarn from the slopes of Great Gable.

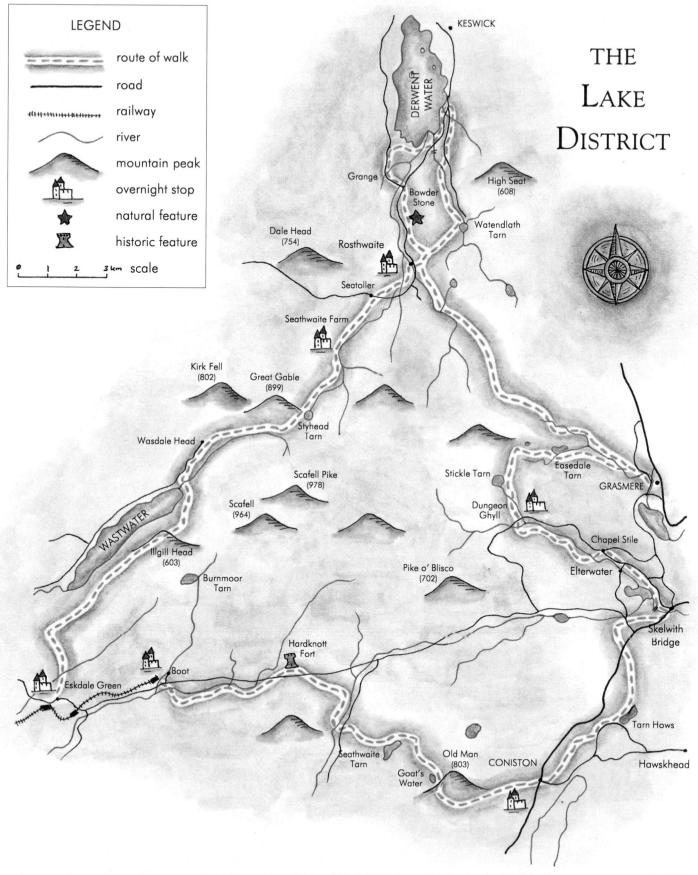

THE
LAKE
DISTRICT

LEGEND

- route of walk
- road
- railway
- river
- mountain peak
- overnight stop
- natural feature
- historic feature

0 1 2 3 km scale

KESWICK

DERWENT WATER

Grange

High Seat
(608)

Bowder Stone

Dale Head
(754)

Rosthwaite

Watendlath Tarn

Seatoller

Seathwaite Farm

Kirk Fell
(802)

Great Gable
(899)

Styhead Tarn

Wasdale Head

Scafell Pike
(978)

Stickle Tarn

Easedale Tarn

GRASMERE

Dungeon Ghyll

WASTWATER

Scafell
(964)

Illgill Head
(603)

Chapel Stile

Elterwater

Burnmoor Tarn

Pike o' Blisco
(702)

Skelwith Bridge

Hardknott Fort

Eskdale Green

Boot

Tarn Hows

Seathwaite Tarn

Old Man
(803)

CONISTON

Hawskhead

Goat's Water

127

Many Lakeland villages have preserved their Victorian charm.

beneath Kirk Fell, Great Gable and Lingmell, only gained electricity in 1979. It has long been a retreat for climbers, many of whom rest permanently in the tiny graveyard.

Continue on the lane to Burnthwaite Farm where you pick up a track which follows Lingmell Beck. Keep along the edge of this, ignoring two paths forking off to the left. The path climbs gradually and then zigzags steeply up to Sty Head. At the top of the pass is a first aid box marking a major junction: a path left ascends Great Gable, another right leads to the Scafells. Instead, keep straight on and descend to Styhead Tarn. Sty Head, meaning 'the top of the ladder', was once on the packhorse route between Borrowdale and Wasdale. The tarn is a dramatic place, quite remote from roads and settlement, with an impressive mountain backdrop. *Once you have rested, continue on the path which follows Styhead Gill downhill. Where the path forks, do not cross the river but keep left of the Gill. Presently you enter a wooded ravine featuring the delightful Taylorgill Force. At the bottom of the valley, turn right and cross the river (which is now the Derwent) over a bridge then continue along this lane to reach Seathwaite Farm. If you can't get accommodation here, continue on to Seatoller, 2 km away.*

DAY TWO - SEATHWAITE FARM TO ROSTHWAITE (18 KM; 6 HRS)

Today's loop route follows flatter ground through beautiful Borrowdale to the picturesque shores of Derwent Water. You should consider leaving overnight luggage in Rosthwaite as you pass through, and just carrying gear for the day and provisions for a picnic lunch.

Leave Seathwaite and turn left to walk 2 km along the road to Seatoller, a hamlet built to house workers from the Honister slate quarries. From here, take a path E and skirt around a wood to reach the River Derwent. Follow this a short distance, then cross a bridge and take a path left through fields to Rosthwaite. Pass through the village and leave it by crossing Stonethwaite Beck. Take a lane left which leads uphill skirting woodland. After 750 m or so, turn left at a footpath signposted to Keswick and the Bowder Stone. This descends through woods to reach a road where you turn right. Some 400 m further on, turn right at a sign to the Bowder Stone. This huge boulder, deposited by a melting glacier and thought to weigh over 2000 tonnes, can be climbed by a ladder.

Continue on past the impressive stone to rejoin the Borrowdale road and follow it N, with good views of High Spy and Maiden Moor up to your left. Turn left over the old bridge which crosses the Derwent and walk through the pretty hamlet of Grange. Stay on this lane as it heads N for 1 km then turn right at a footpath signposted to Lodore. This crosses marshy grazing land and bears E along the head of the beautiful Derwent Water. Cross the river once more and soon turn left onto the road. Just past the Lodore Swiss Hotel (where you can detour to the Lodore Cascades), pick up a parallel path through Strutta Wood and reach the road at a car park. Past this, turn left onto a lakeside path which soon rejoins the road at Ashness Landing Stage. Climb some steps away from the lake and take the lane straight on signposted Ashness Bridge and Watendlath.

Cross this old packhorse bridge and look back for the famous view of the lake and Derwent Fells beyond. This is surpassed by a viewpoint from a ledge 800 m further along the lane from where the scene of Derwent Water, Bassenthwaite and the looming Skiddaw is quite magnificent. *From here, continue on a footpath parallel to the lane. At a wall climb a stile and turn right over Watendlath Beck then turn left to follow the beck for over 2 km, first through woods and then over meadows below crags to Watendlath, a delightful hamlet set at the junction of several ancient tracks.* The stone farm buildings are now owned by the National Trust, as is much of the countryside over which you have passed this afternoon. *Bear right to pass Watendlath Tarn and then, at a fork, go uphill to Rosthwaite on the bridletrack, a former packhorse route to Thirlmere. It climbs to a pass and then descends to Borrowdale providing charming views. At the Resting Stone, where you diverted this morning, take the left forking path down past Hazel Bank to Rosthwaite.* This is a small village with a general store, a hotel, a hostel and numerous B&Bs.

Day Three - Rosthwaite to Great Langdale (20 km; 7.5 hrs)

This morning you pick up the Coast to Coast path, a waymarked long distance path pioneered by A.F.Wainwright, the doyen of Lakeland walkers and writers. This passes through Stonethwaite Valley, an exquisitely preserved stretch of farmland, over remote Greenup Gill to reach pretty Grasmere after 11.75 km for lunch. The way continues, via several spectacular tarns, for the dramatic valley of Great Langdale.

A dramatic view across Derwent Water to Cat Bells and Causey Pike.

Leave Rosthwaite by crossing back over Stonethwaite Beck and turning right onto a gravel lane, through a gate at the beck and along the lane. Do not cross Stonethwaite Bridge, but continue on in the same direction along the beck. After 1 km or so, you reach the pretty junction of Langstrath Beck and Greenup Gill where the Cumbria Way diverges south for Stake Pass. Stay on the east bank of Greenup Gill and follow it uphill, between the imposing heights of Long Band and Eagle Crag (named when golden eagles were common here). The path climbs steeply to Lining Crag, then reaches Greenup Edge at 600 m. This is a wild and lonely place, but the path is over easy ground. Continue on, descending southeast to the head of Far Easedale Gill. The path crosses this twice as it descends. (Don't detour here to Easedale Tarn, as you will visit it later.) *Eventually, you reach a lane which leads into Grasmere.*

Grasmere, nestling in its natural amphitheatre in the very heart of the Lakes, is a charming village which is understandably popular with visitors. Dove Cottage, the home of William Wordsworth, lies a short stroll beyond the village near Grasmere Lake. *Leave Grasmere by the lane to Easedale. Where it veers right, cross Easedale Beck and pick up a path which follows the beck uphill. At the junction of Far Easedale Gill and Sour Milk Gill, the path steepens as you follow the latter up to Easedale Tarn.* A stone hut here once served refreshments to the Victorian tourists who walked from Grasmere.

Follow the path around the south of the tarn, crossing a stream which feeds into it. The route between here and Stickle Tarn is not much used and you should take care as it is rocky in places. Follow the path as it climbs steeply up onto Slapestone Edge, passing the small Codale Tarn. 300 m from Codale Tarn, turn left onto a path that heads south, descending to Stickle Tarn and skirting along its eastern bank. This sheet of water is set dramatically at the base of Paveys Ark and Harrison Stickle. To the south, across Great Langdale, stands the conical Lingmoor Fell. *The path descends steeply beside Stickle Ghyll (ghyll is a fanciful version of* gill)*, past its several waterfalls, to reach the Great Langdale road at the New Dungeon Ghyll Hotel.* Along the road are several hotels and farms offering B&B accommodation. The Old Dungeon Ghyll Hotel has been giving shelter to climbers and walkers for around 300 years.

DAY FOUR - GREAT LANGDALE TO CONISTON (18 KM; 6 HRS)

Today's journey joins the Cumbria Way long distance path from Great Langdale to Coniston, via the delightful Tarn Hows. Lunch can be bought at Skelwith Bridge. If time permits, you might consider a detour to the pretty village of Hawkshead along the way.

From the New Dungeon Ghyll Hotel, walk down the lane to the main road. Turn right and after 150 m or so, turn left onto a footpath which soon crosses Great Langdale Beck to reach Side House Farm. The path climbs and heads east, then contours around the fell and follows the beck to Oak Howe, once a farm. Take the path left down to the beck and follow the right bank for a further 1 km then cross a bridge and follow a track as it veers right, passes Thrang Farm and reaches the main road near the village of Chapel Stile. Turn right onto the road and after some 50 m, cross the beck by a footbridge and follow the riverside

Dungeon Ghyll Force, one of the more curiously named features of the Lakes.

The village of Chapel Stile,
just off the path in the valley
of Great Langdale.

path which becomes a surfaced road. *Turn left over a bridge to the small village
of Elterwater.* This was once a centre for burning charcoal which was then
used to make gunpowder, a major industry here in the 18th century. *Take a
path right and follow the beck downstream to Elter Water, the Norse rendition of
'lake of the swans'. Continue on the track which runs between the main road and
the River Brathay (which eventually feeds into Windermere). Pass the dramatic
falls of Skelwith Force and walk through a slateworks to reach Skelwith Bridge
village.* Slate has been quarried around this area for centuries and is still
vital to the local economy. Several establishments nearby offer a restoring
lunch.

*Rich pasture lies beneath the fells
of the Lake District.*

Cross the River Brathay and follow the road to Coniston for 100 m, before picking up a clear woodland path which follows the road and then veers W to Elterwater Park. Continue on, past Low Park and cross a stile to reach a road. Turn right and, before you reach Colwith Bridge, turn left onto a track which climbs through woodland to High Park. Turn left onto a road which leads, after 1 km, back to the Coniston road. Follow this south for 500 m then take the rough road which forks left uphill. Contour around a hill and then take a right forking footpath through forest to Tarn Hows. Originally, there were several small tarns hereabouts, but in 1916 a local landowner had them linked and planted conifers to create the attractive landscape that exists today. At the end of the tarn pick up a road which shortly reaches a junction.

For a detour to the limewashed village of Hawkshead (home to a Beatrix Potter museum and to Wordsworth's school), turn left and, at the tarn's eastern edge, pick up a path to Hawkshead Hill from where another path descends through fields to the village. The diversion to Hawkshead and back adds 6.5 km to your walk. Alternatively, turn left at the junction then right onto a contouring road. Take a lane right to Tarn Hows Cottages and continue W on a path that leads downhill through wood to Yewdale Beck. Follow the beck past a bridge, then turn right through a field. Go through a gateway at a junction and continue straight on for 250 m to a stile and into a wood, gaining a wonderful view down to Coniston Water. Descend and cross the beck at Shepherd Bridge. Turn left onto the road and then right at a junction into Coniston.

Coniston derives its name from the Anglo-Saxon for 'king's village' and it has a certain majesty, set between the long sheet of Coniston Water and craggy peaks of the Coniston fells. It has a long mining history, the area being rich in copper, iron and slate. Across the lake (on a ferry route) is Brantwood, the home of the artist and writer John Ruskin. Coniston is well served with accommodation.

DAY FIVE - CONISTON TO BOOT (19.5 KM; 7 HRS)

Today's walk takes you through remote countryside, past the seldom visited Goat's Water and Seathwaite Tarn (take provisions for a picnic lunch hereabouts), on to the dramatically situated Roman fort on Hardknott Pass and then down to Boot. This pretty village is at the end of the Eskdale scenic railway, so you can return to Eskdale Green if you choose.

Leave Coniston by a road which climbs sharply to what was once the terminus of a rail line. Continue uphill for 1.25 km to a junction. If the weather is good and you have both time and energy, you could turn right here and climb Coniston Old Man then continue down to Goats Hause and pick up the track there. *Otherwise, continue straight ahead on the Walna Scar track for 1.75 km.* This track has long been used for carrying out the slate quarried at various sites nearby. Down to the left of the track, important Bronze Age relics were discovered. *Just after a natural rock gateway, branch off to the right on a track which rises to a hollow known as The Cove. The path rises to reach Goat's Water, backed by the massive precipices of Dow Crag. Follow the path along the east bank of the tarn, then ascend to reach a slight dip known as Goat's Hause (a hause is a pass).*

Cross the traversing footpath and descend along Far Gill to cross a beck and pass disused copper mines (which are dangerous to enter). The path follows around the northern shore of Seathwaite Tarn and then reaches a beck. Do not cross it, but continue west to Foss How. Pick up a path that branches to the right and follow this down to Pike How. Turn left onto the road and, after 500 m, cross Birks Bridge. This crosses the River Duddon which can rise swiftly in floods and has scoured out rockpools below the packhorse bridge.

Turn right on a riverside path and follow the beautiful river for 1.5 km, then veer left towards Black Hall Farm. Just before the farm buildings, turn sharp left through a gate and cross a field. Pass through a gap in a wall and follow the wall left for almost 100 m, then bear right and climb a rough grassy slope. Head to the trees, keeping just to the right of the boundary wall. Continue uphill, climbing a stile over another wall. Past the end of the trees you reach the top of the ridge with a wonderful view of Eskdale. Veer slightly right and descend to the road near the top of the notoriously steep and winding Hardknott Pass and turn left onto the road; take care here as drivers will no doubt be distracted. At a hairpin bend to the left keep straight on along a faint path to Mediobognum. Mediobognum, better known as Hardknott Fort, was a strategic defence post built by the Romans at the beginning of the 2nd century AD. The layout of the complex, which comprised barracks, bath houses, a granary and parade ground, is still visible and it is a sobering thought to imagine the harsh life

The Roman fort of Mediobognum was established to fend off attacks launched from the sea.

of the 500 soldiers sent here to defend this outpost of the Roman Empire. Leave the fort from the western end and continue along the road. At the bottom of the hill, branch off to the left onto a lane which leads down the valley, south of the River Esk. Cross the river at Doctor Bridge (a 17th century packhorse bridge widened later by a local doctor to accommodate his horse and trap) and follow along its north bank until you reach the isolated parish church, where you turn right onto a lane that brings you soon to the pleasant village of Boot. Dalegarth railway station is a short walk down the road towards Eskdale Green.

NOTES ON THE LAKE DISTRICT

TYPE OF WALK	Circular (with a short rail connection)
LENGTH OF WALK	94.5 kilometres (59 miles); five days
DIFFICULTY	An energetic walk, with long days
START	Eskdale Green, in the Western Lakes
FINISH	Boot, a short distance from Eskdale Green by rail

PUBLIC TRANSPORT
Eskdale Green is serviced by train from Ravenglass (Irton Road station). Dalegarth station at Boot is a short distance down this line. Local buses can be used to shorten the walk if bad weather strikes. For information, telephone the Cumbria Journey Planner Enquiry Line on 01228) 606000.

LUGGAGE   Leave excess luggage at Eskdale Green.

CLIMATE
The weather in the Lake District is notoriously wet and unpredictable; even on a fine day be prepared for mist, heavy rain and wind. May to September are the best months for walking with longer hours of daylight and warmer temperatures. Snow falls on the peaks in winter.

MAP   Ordnance Survey (OS) Outdoor Leisure Nos. 4,5,6 and 7 *The English Lakes* 1:25,000

PATH   This route includes short stretches of the Cumbria Way and the Coast to Coast Path, both of which are waymarked. The route also includes woodland tracks and unwaymarked footpaths.

SHORTER VARIANT   (see Days 5 & 1)
Two-day version: *Train to Windermere, bus to Coniston;* 1 - walk from Coniston to Boot; *train to Eskdale Green;* 2 - walk from Eskdale Green to Seathwaite farm; *bus from Seatoller to Keswick, thence Windermere.*

VILLAGES
Eskdale Green (population <150), **Seathwaite** (<100), Seatoller (<100), Watendlath (<100), **Rosthwaite** (<150), Grasmere (app.2000), **Dungeon Ghyll** (<100), Elterwater (<150), Skelwith Bridge (<100), **Coniston** (app.2800), **Boot** (<100).

ACCOMMODATION

The region caters well for walkers: even small villages offer accommodation in pubs and B&Bs. All of the overnight stops, with the exception of Coniston, have limited places to stay. If you are travelling in mid-summer, book ahead.

CUISINE

Cumbria is renowned for its Cumberland ham and Cumberland pork sausage. Grasmere boasts a shop which makes wonderful gingerbread to an old recipe. Kendal Mint Cake, a solid sweet slab which is popular as a source of energy for walkers, originates in the District.

WILDLIFE

The endangered red squirrel and golden eagle survive here in small numbers. Native deer such as the red deer and roe deer are also to be found, as are badgers and foxes. Birdlife includes peregrines, sparrow hawks and merlins as well as moorland birds such as curlews and golden plover.

SPECIAL FEATURES

Glacial lakes such as Wastwater (England's deepest) and Derwent Water; numerous mountain tarns, streams and waterfalls, including Dungeon Ghyll Force and Skelwith Force; dramatic passes between England's highest mountains; the bucolic valleys of Wasdale, Borrowdale, Stonethwaite, Great Langdale and Eskdale; the Roman fort at Hardknott Pass.

FURTHER READING

WAINWRIGHT ON THE LAKELAND MOUNTAIN PASSES, FELLWALKING WITH WAINWRIGHT and WAINWRIGHT'S FAVOURITE LAKELAND MOUNTAINS
by A.Wainwright, photographs by Derry Brabbs, published by Michael Joseph

LAKE DISTRICT WALKS and MORE LAKE DISTRICT WALKS
Ordnance Survey Pathfinder Guides

100 LAKE DISTRICT HILL WALKS
by Gordon Brown, published by Sigma

USEFUL ADDRESSES

RAMBLER'S ASSOCIATION
1/5 Wandsworth Road, London SW8 2LJ; Tel: 0171) 5826878

PARK INFORMATION CENTRE (PIC)
Keswick, Tel: 017687) 72803

CUMBRIA TOURIST BOARD
Ashleigh, Holly Rd, Windermere, Cumbria LA23 2AQ; Tel: 015394) 44444   Fax: 015394) 44041
Internet address: www.cumbria-the-lake-district.co.uk

THE BERNESE ALPS

A choice of spectacular alpine day walks above the Lauterbrunnental, a picture-perfect glacial valley set amid lofty glacial peaks, mountain meadows and feathery waterfalls.

To walkers, Switzerland means Alps and few Alpine peaks are better known than the Eiger, Mönch and Jungfrau trio located in the Bernese Alps. The spectacular Bernese Alps are a rugged range of mountain giants (the highest in the Alps apart from the main continental divide) which separates the German-speaking Bern canton from the French-speaking Valais to the south. With north-south access confined to a few often snowbound mountain passes, the Bernese Alps constitute both a geographical and cultural divide. At over 4000 metres, the summits of the Jungfrau and its neighbours are the domain of the mountaineer; to their south lies an arctic wilderness of permanent ice from which arises the Grosser Aletsch-gletscher, the Alps' largest icefield. To their west and north however, the slopes and glacial valleys high above the twin lakes of Thunersee and Brienzersee are a walker's heaven. Here is a landscape of delightful contrast: a backdrop of snowcapped summits, blue-tinged glaciers and sheer waterfalls with a foreground of forest, foaming torrents and flower-strewn meadowland.

Our collection of varied day walks is based around the pretty village of Lauterbrunnen in the heart of the Lauterbrunnental, an exquisite U-shaped glacial valley through which courses the Weisse Lütschine. The name of Lauterbrunnen (*clear springs*) refers to the more than 60 waterfalls which cascade down the valley's sheer walls, including the ten-stage Trümmelbach Falls, viewed from inside the mountain, and the famous Staubbach Falls on Lauterbrunnen's outskirts. In the middle ages the valley was settled by Walliser farmers (that is, from the Valais) who built on the high terraces rather than the flood-prone valley floor. The villages of Wengen, Mürren, Gimmelwald, Stechelberg and Isenfluh all date from this farming migration and, while modern tourism has brough prosperity, the land continues to be farmed traditionally, assisted by generous subsidy. Meadows are hand-mown with scythes and the tinkle of cow bells is often heard near *alp* or high pasture. The area's prosperity is reflected in its Swiss chalet architecture. Tiny wooden barns are dark with the patina of age and large, ornately carved farm buildings are bedecked with window boxes of geraniums.

Alpine rhododendron adds a splash of colour to the Tanzbödeli meadowland, high in the Lauterbrunnen valley.

*The waterfall-lined walls of
the glacial Lauterbrunnental.*

*The Eiger's north face,
overlooking Kleine Scheidegg.*

Such a beautiful region is inevitably well touristed but leave the resorts and mountain transport behind and even in peak season you might find yourself alone on some of these walks. This need not cause concern as the trails are extremely well waymarked. Fingerboard signs are prolific: yellow diamond metal waymarks indicate low-level *wanderweg* routes; red-and-white stripe waymarks denote *bergweg* mountain routes, usually more strenuous. The Lauterbrunnental is served by an amazing network of funiculars, gondolas, cog-railways and postbuses and our walks utilise these to gain initial altitude. Even so, none of the walks described is graded easy, though there is ample easy rambling to be found here. The truth is that here the choicest walking does require a commitment of time and some exertion but the rewards are exceptional!

WALK ONE - THE KLEINE SCHEIDEGG (11 KM; 3.5 HRS)

This wonderful medium-grade walk provides a classic close-up of the Eiger's north face as well as panoramic views of the beautiful Lauterbrunnental. You could conveniently undertake this walk after an excursion on Europe's highest railway which tunnels through the Eiger to the Sphinx observatory at 3454 m on the Jungfraujoch saddle.

From Lauterbrunnen, take the cog railway to Kleine Scheidegg (literally little watershed*), a 2061 m pass and a station on the famous Jungfraujoch railway line.* Before leaving Kleine Scheidegg's throngs, savour the direct views of the Jungfrau and Mönch and of course the notorious Eiger Nordwand: telescopes enable you to follow the progress of any rock climbers. The 4 km route to the 2229 m Männlichen hotel is a gently ascending ridge walk north through flower-filled alpine meadows on a broad and clearly marked path. Walking on the Grindelwald side of the ridge, you curve beneath the Lauberhorn and later the Tschuggen with superb views down to Grindelwald and beyond to the Wetterhorn and Schreckhorn. *Past the hotel and restaurant continue up the ridge path to the Männlichen summit (2343 m).* Here are magnificent views: the Lauterbrunnental beneath you; to the south the Jungfrau and its snowcapped neighbours.

Return to the hotel (gondola to Grindelwald/Grund; cable-car to Wengen); nearby the 4 km path for Wengen takes you over the ridge's west side and beneath the cable-car before making a steep and zigzagging descent (a 950 m height loss) with more views of the Lauterbrunnental. The path passes the avalanche fences visible from the valley floor before reaching a path junction at Parwengi (1864 m) where there is a choice of routes to Wengen. Take the right fork which winds down steeply to the alp huts of Ussri-Allmi and hence into Wengen from the north. Wengen (1275 m) is a pretty, car-free resort village occupying a sunny terrace high above Lauterbrunnen. *At Wengen's railway station find the signposted trail down to Lauterbrunnen. The route passes under the railway and onto a minor road with a view of the Staubbach falls. Soon descend steeply through forest, crossing the railway twice more. Emerging from the forest, descend past some chalets before crossing the footbridge over the torrential Weisse Lütschine and finally reaching Lauterbrunnen's railway station.*

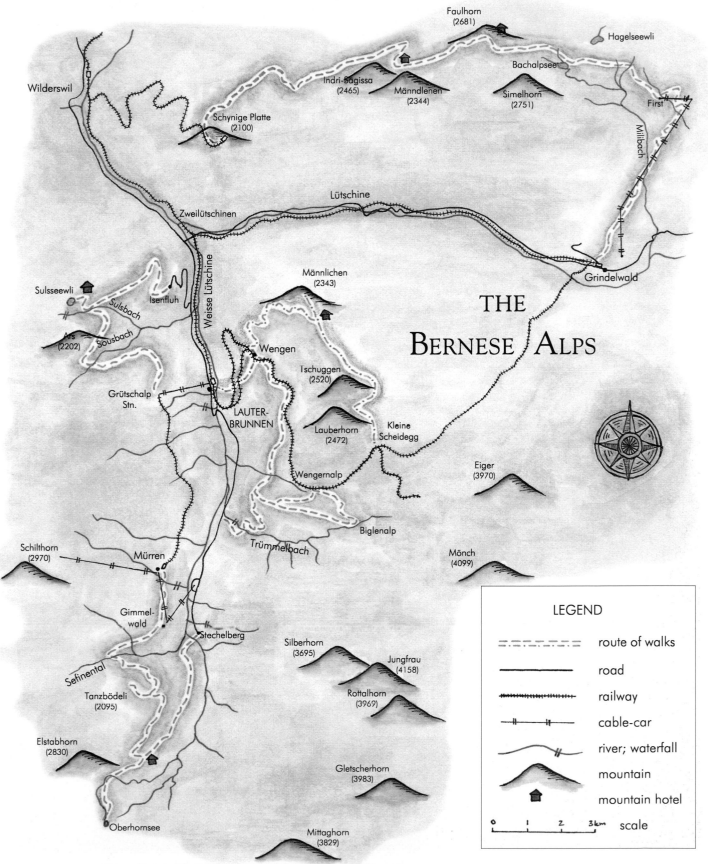

Faulhorn
(2681)

Hagelseewli

Bachalpsee

Indri-Sägissa
(2465)

Männdlenen
(2344)

Simelhorn
(2751)

First

Milibach

Wilderswil

Schynige Platte
(2100)

Lütschine

Zweilütschinen

Grindelwald

THE

BERNESE ALPS

Sulsseewli

Isenfluh

Männlichen
(2343)

Sulsbach

Weisse Lütschine

Wengen

Ars
(2202)

Sousbach

Ischuggen
(2520)

Grütschalp
Stn.

LAUTER-
BRUNNEN

Lauberhorn
(2472)

Kleine
Scheidegg

Eiger
(3970)

Wengernalp

Biglenalp

Schilthorn
(2970)

Mürren

Trümmelbach

Mönch
(4099)

Gimmel-
wald

LEGEND

Stechelberg

Silberhorn
(3695)

Jungfrau
(4158)

Sefinental

Rottalhorn
(3969)

Tanzbödeli
(2095)

Elstabhorn
(2830)

Gletscherhorn
(3983)

Oberhornsee

Mittaghorn
(3829)

route of walks

road

railway

cable-car

river; waterfall

mountain

mountain hotel

0   1   2   3 km   scale

139

WALK TWO - SOUSTAL AND THE SULSSEEWLI (10 KM; 4 HRS)

This medium grade walk high above the Lauterbrunnental's west wall has everything: secluded back valleys, waterfalls, a hidden tarn and an idyllic mountain hut with magnificent mountain vistas thrown in.

Take the funicular from Lauterbrunnen to Grütschalp where you should pause to take in the views of the Eiger, Mönch and Jungfrau. Cross the rail tracks and ascend the signposted path roughly north. Go right at a fork, through a gate and take the left fork to enter a working forest. Ascending gently, you contour a hill, at one point gaining an impressive view of the distant Sousbach Falls. Descend to Sousläger where there is a drinking trough and cross the Sousbach on a footbridge. You are now in the lower Soustal, a pastoral backwater with delightful views up valley towards the Spaltenhorn. *Over the bridge, veer left at a track junction and climb on a steep, switchback path (or continue upstream for a longer but gentler alternative ascent), pausing to look back as views of the Wyssbirg open up. The path now slowly contours around a spur of the Ars.* Looking back, you can see the Schilthorn summit with its famous revolving restaurant, Piz Gloria and eventually you gain 270° views as the narrow Sulstal comes into view. *Descend and cross the Sulsbach on the Fritzebruggli bridge and at a path junction, head left upstream to the alp of Suls.* Here is a captivating scene: an isolated farmhouse and cattle byres set amid meadow and alpine flowers, beneath a circle of mountains and a waterfall. From here it is some 5 minutes to the Sulsseewli tarn in another superb location.

The big three: Ogre, Monk and Maiden.

A few minutes past the tarn, at a signed junction, turn right and ascend to the Lobhörnhutte (beds and refreshments) past strangely fissured limestone pavement. The hut's outdoor terrace offers a superb vantage point: to the south, the Jungfrau and its neighbours; southwest, the five fingers of the Lobhörner and closer, the onion-skin face of the Ars. It is an ideal place to lunch.

Descend from the hut on another path marked to Sulsalp, heading directly towards the waterfall. Reach the Sulsbach path at the alp and follow it downstream. Past the bridge it diverges left from the stream, descending through meadowland (wonderful views up to the Wetterhorn as well as the big three) and later through forest. The path crosses a road signed to Mederalp and continues on down to Sulwald (1520 m), a picturesque hamlet from where you can ride a cable-car down to Isenfluh (1084 m) saving one hour's steep descent. Alternatively, the winding forest path descent is well signposted to Isenfluh where a postbus leaves for Lauterbrunnen. If planning to walk back to Lauterbrunnen check beforehand that the footpath is not closed due to rockfall.

WALK THREE - BIGLENALP AND THE TRÜMMELTAL (14.5 KM; 6 HRS)

This is easy walking through beautiful Biglenalp above Wengen to confront the Eiger's glaciers, followed by a more difficult route down the steep gully of the Trümmelbach to the Lauterbrunnental. This walk could be followed by a visit to the famous Trümmelbach Falls. Take lunch supplies.

Take the train from Lauterbrunnen to Wengen. From the railway station follow the sign for Wengernalp. Turn right under the railway line, then gradually climb to reach a junction where you take the lower fork signposted to Wengernalp and Biglenalp. The broad farm track rises easily through mixed pasture and forest. Keep ahead at the next junction (Langentrejen, 1600 m), taking in the views back down to Wengen and left above you to the Männlichen-Lauberhorn ridge. At a signed and gated junction (Staldenfluh, 1681 m) ignore the right fork downhill (you take this later), continuing on the main track. Past farm buildings at Mettlenalp (1725 m), where the track curves around up left, take the path ahead signed to Biglenalp. Exiting the forest near Biglenalp farm, the prospect is delightful, with close-up views ahead to the imposing Jungfrau massif and right across the Lauterbrunnental to the green terrace of Mürren. You may see and hear the small avalanches of ice which the Jungfrau sheds during the summer melt. To the left are the Guggigletscher and Eigergletscher: they feed Biglenalp's pretty stream which becomes the ferocious Trümmelbach below. No better spot for a picnic could be imagined!

To continue to Wengernalp, don't bridge the stream as the map suggests; instead veer left uphill on a path signed to Weissefluh and Wengernalp. At Weissefluh (1835 m) continue ahead for nearby Wixi, a skilift base, where you turn left. Pass a farmhouse at Wengernalp where produce and refreshments are available. In The Playground of Europe, Leslie Stephen wrote "Surely the Wengern Alp must be precisely the loveliest place in this world." With its wildflower-strewn meadows and mountain backdrop, it is indeed a superb location though perhaps Leslie Stephen never reached Biglenalp. The train from Wengernalp station allows for a quick return to Wengen and Lauter-

A view of the Ars from the Lobhörnhutte.

Biglenalp, on the lower slopes of the Jungfrau.

*The Trümmelbach commences
its mountain descent.*

*The quaint alpine salamander can be
some compensation for wet weather.*

brunnen. *Otherwise, turn left downhill on a path signed to Mettlenalp. Zigzag down steeply into woodland and turn right onto a track and soon after, left onto a footpath marked with a yellow diamond sign. The path joins a track and soon you are back at Mettlenalp from where you retrace your steps to Staldenfluh.*

Take a path signed to Trümmelbach which zigzags down left to soon go left at another junction. You are now on a *bergweg* (red-and-white stripe waymarks) and the descent ahead is precipitous with an 800 m height loss. Though there are fixed metal chains and ladders to assist the descent, you need to be sure-footed. To compensate, you gain unique views down the Trümmeltal to Gimmelwald and Stechelberg. *After a very steep descent through forest, carefully cross a slippery wooden bridge over the raging Trümmelbach. Below, it plunges into a chasm to commence its plummet within the mountain as the Trümmelbach Falls. After a short steep ascent, there is another lengthy zigzagging descent, steep in places, with metal rope to assist in sections. The path comes out where the Trümmelbach emerges from the mountain. Walk alongside the torrent to reach the road just south of the Trümmelbach Falls entrance and bus stop. Either catch the postbus back to Lauterbrunnen or pick up the charming footpath to Lauterbrunnen a little further along the road.*

WALK FOUR - TANZBÖDELI AND OBERHORNSEE (17 KM; 8 HRS)

Today's tough but hugely rewarding hike takes you over the Sefinental's south ridge to the high Tanzbödeli meadow and then to a hidden tarn deep in the Lauterbrunnen back valley. Start early and carry lunch!

The walk begins at Mürren, reached from Lauterbrunnen by funicular to Grütschalp where you change for the spectacular narrow-gauge train ride. Car-free Mürren (1639 m) occupies a sunny terrace 800 m above the Lauterbrunnental and commands incomparable views of valley and massif. *From here it is a 30 minute, signposted walk by road and steps down to Gimmelwald (1363 m),* a time-forgotten village whose 'avalanche zoning' has prevented development. *Follow 'Obersteinberg' signs, on road then track, down towards the Sefinental. Descend to cross the raging Sefinen Lütschine on a bergweg. Now it is a long steep climb out of the Sefinental, initially through the Busewald. Break the climb frequently for views back to Gimmelwald and beyond to Mürren. Go through a gate and up through meadow to a junction where you take the left fork marked to Oberhornsee and veer left again at the idyllic Unter Busenalp. Continue uphill to a path junction on the Busengrat ridge spur. If time permits, detour right uphill for 20 minutes to have lunch atop the Tanzbödeli meadowland (2095 m).* Here you enjoy a 360° panorama 1200 m above valley, taking in the Schilthorn, Ellstabhorn, Gspaltenhorn, Tschingelhorn, Jungfrau and others. *Back at Busengrat go right on a path contouring along exposed hillside and descend to the Obersteinberg mountain hotel (accommodation and meals).*

Pick up the path SW for Oberhornsee. Climb steadily and cross the Tschingel Lütschine on a wooden bridge: take care if crossing late lying snow. A final ascent reveals the tarn. The tiny, deep blue Oberhornsee (2065 m) is set amid a wild terrain of boulders and moraine, beneath the Breithorn and Tschingelhorn whose sides are hung with glaciers. The views are breathtaking. You

Oberhornsee, a tiny glacial tarn perched high in the back Lauterbrunnental.

are now deep in the back Lauterbrunnental, once a mining area and now a nature reserve rich in geological diversity where the flora and fauna are protected and farming is carried out in traditional manner. You should see marmots beyond the lake and perhaps the golden eagle which preys on them; chamois and even ibex occasionally visit the high precipices.

Retrace your steps to Obersteinberg from where there is a choice of routes down valley to Stechelberg. Recommended is the higher path via Hotel Tschingelhorn (offering meals and accommodation) where you continue ahead into forest at a fork. The way down to Stechelberg is straightforward though steep in places with a great view of the Schmadribach Falls' 400 m plume. Catch the postbus back to Lauterbrunnen. Otherwise it is a level 7 km walk back on farm roads.

WALK FIVE - SCHYNIGE PLATTE TO GRINDELWALD (23 KM; 6 HRS)

One of the Alps' classics, this high-level traverse of the ridge separating the Brienzersee from the Jungfrau region offers wonderful views over lakes and mountains. The walk is long and moderately strenuous despite the use of transport to gain height. Save this one for promising weather! *Take an early train to Wilderswil and, from there, the historic (1893) cog-railway to Schynige Platte (1967 m) where the Alpengarten may be visited. From the station take the path signed to Oberberghorn and at a nearby junction follow the longer alternative route to Oberberghorn, aptly signed 'Panoramaweg'. Presently you reach a fork where you can detour left to gain the Oberberghorn summit*

The final walk takes you to the neighbouring valley of Grindelwald.

(2069 m) *utilising wooden ladders which are slippery when wet.* Along the path and particularly from the summit you gain dramatic views down to Brienzersee, Interlaken and Thunersee. This area is a haven for alpine salamanders which venture onto the path in moist conditions.

Back at the junction, take the Panoramaweg to Laucheren from where you contour around the scree of the Loucherhorn's western and southern flanks. Now the geology changes, with limestone cliffs and boulders dominating the landscape as you cross the minor col of Egg (2067 m) to the head of the little cirque of Sägistal, a sheep-grazed valley with its own tarn. The path climbs gently, contouring above the Sägistalsee (anticipate late-lying snow) and below the Indri-Sägissa before looping back up through a karstic landscape to reach the Männdlenen saddle. Here sits the tiny Webberhutte, offering meals and mattresses. *Take the path to Faulhorn, climbing steeply up rock steps and then more easily along the Winteregg ridge with views of the Faulhorn ahead and new views of the Eiger, Mönch and Jungfrau. The main path skirts just below the Berghotel Faulhorn and the Faulhorn summit (2680 m).* Make the detour: the Faulhorn's panoramic views of the Jungfrau range and down to Brienzersee are among the best in the Swiss Alps and the hotel is the oldest Alpine mountain hotel.

You now make a 400 m descent via the Gassenboden saddle (2553 m) and past an emergency shelter into the Bachalpsee basin. The Bachalpsee is actually two connected tarns, cradled by grassy slopes and draining into the Milibach. From its northern edge is seen one of the classic Alpine panoramas with the awesome, glacier-clad summits of Schreckhorn, Finsteraarhorn and Fiescherhorn reflected in serene waters. *Take a gravel track (the upper trail) above the second lake and begin to descend high above the Milibach. Look out for the marmot colony below and for chamois above on the ridge to your left. Follow signs to the upper gondola station at First (2167 m) where you can either take the gondola (check the time of final descent beforehand) or walk down to Grindelwald on steep mountain roads amid the sublime scenery of the Grindelwald basin. From Grindelwald return by train to Lauterbrunnen.*

Notes on the Bernese Alps

TYPE OF WALK	Day walks from one base
LENGTH OF WALK	75.5 kilometres (47 miles) over five days
DIFFICULTY	Ranging from medium to hard grade, with steep ascents and descents
START	Lauterbrunnen, set in the beautiful glacial valley of Lauterbrunnental

PUBLIC TRANSPORT
Lauterbrunnen is on the railway; change at Interlaken Ost.
Yellow postbuses run between Lauterbrunnen and both Stechelberg and Isenfluh regularly.

CLIMATE
Snow can stay on the ground until June. Afternoon thunderstorms are common in early summer and the most settled weather occurs in autumn. The walking season is from June to late October.

MAP   Landeskarte der Schweitz 5004 *Berner Oberland* 1:50,000

PATH   Footpaths waymarked with yellow signposts and some red-and-white stripe markings.

VILLAGES
Lauterbrunnen (population 1010), Wengen (1050), Mürren (350), Stechelberg (300), Gimmelwald (130), Isenfluh (75), Grindelwald (3850).

ACCOMMODATION
Lauterbrunnen has numerous hotels and *pensions*, as well as several *matratzenlagers* (inns with dormitaries).

CUISINE
Cheeses such as Gruyère and Emmentaler, are the basis for many classic Swiss dishes. These include *fondue* (a melted mixture of various cheeses, wine and garlic), *raclette* (grilled cheeses with pickles) and *rösti* (a pan-fried dish of potato).

WILDLIFE
Colonies of marmots live above the treeline in the high valleys. Herds of chamois and (less commonly) ibex can be seen on the higher slopes. Alpine flowers bloom in abundance between June and October.

SPECIAL FEATURES
Numerous dramatic waterfalls, including the Staubbach and Trümmelbach; views of the Jungfrau and surrounding mountains; the mountain tarns of Sulsseewli, Oberhornsee and Bachalpsee.

FURTHER READING

THE BERNESE ALPS: A WALKING GUIDE
by Kev Reynolds, published by Cicerone, UK, 1997

WALKING IN SWITZERLAND
by Clem Lindenmayer, published by Lonely Planet, Australia, 1996.

USEFUL ADDRESSES

SCHWEITZER WANDERWEG (SWISS HIKING FEDERATION)
Im Hirschalm 49, CH-4125, Riehen; Tel: 061) 6011535

LAUTERBRUNNEN TOURIST OFFICE
Tel: 855 1955 Fax: 855 3604 email: lauterbrunnen.tourismus@bluewin.ch

INTERNET SITES http://www.berneseoberland.ch   http://www.berneroberland-hotels.ch

THE HIGH ALPUJARRAS

A five-day walk showcasing the exotic white villages which perch on the southern foothills of Spain's highest mountain range, the Sierra Nevada.

Andalucia's Alpujarras offer travellers a number of curious contradictions. From a distance, the land can appear dry and barren; at close quarters it is fertile and sometimes even lush. There are few major edifices to indicate its history, but the countryside is stamped with signs of the various civilisations which have inhabited and shaped it, most markedly the Moors. A trek across its gorges and slopes can be an enlightening experience into the way a culture interacts with a somewhat hostile landscape.

The valleys of the Alpujarras are to the south of the fascinating city of Granada and some mere fifty kilometres north of the tourist-infested Costa del Sol. They lie at the foothills of the Sierra Nevada–literally the 'snowy mountains'–which are indeed perpetually capped in snow. The constant trickle of melting snow transforms into several rivers which, over time, have cut into the mountains' soft shale and mica to form dramatic ravines. Along these rivers, which have deposited a wealth of rich silt and workable soil, a number of small villages have developed, often perched precariously on steep hillsides. These slopes are terraced to retain the fertile river silt, a form of landscaping which was probably begun by the Visigoths or the Ibero-Celts who settled the area some two thousand years ago. The Moors and Berbers, refugees from the reconquest of Sevilla who settled here in the 12th century, continued the tradition of terracing and laid a system of complex *acequias* or water channels which still irrigate the fields today.

The Moorish Muslim population here increased when Granada finally fell to the Christians in 1492, and many of those who withdrew to the Alpujarras, guaranteed freedom of worship by treaty, were later forced to convert to Christianity. These Moriscos, as they were known, rebelled against high taxes and persecution and the Alpujarras were the setting for a bitter struggle in 1568. The Moors were finally expelled from the country, save for a few families forced to remain to show the new settlers from Galicia and Asturias how to manage the acequias and how to breed silkworms. Despite their help, the region was never again as prosperous, and the population dwindled. During the Civil War, the locals were caught somewhat between the Nationalists based in Granada and the Republicans from

The picturesque pueblos biancos *or 'white villages' of the High Alpujarras are unique in Spain.*

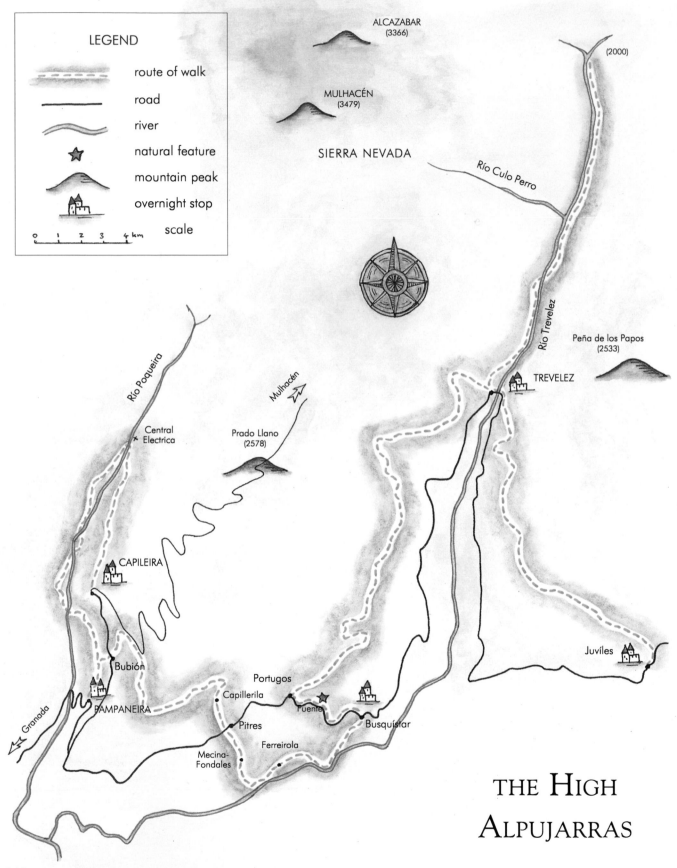

LEGEND

route of walk

road

river

★ natural feature

mountain peak

overnight stop

scale

0 1 2 3 4 km

ALCAZABAR
(3366)

(2000)

MULHACÉN
(3479)

SIERRA NEVADA

Río Culo Perro

Río Poqueira

Río Trevelez

Peña de los Papos
(2533)

Mulhacén

Central
Electrica

Prado Llano
(2578)

TREVELEZ

CAPILEIRA

Bubión

Portugos

Capillerila

Juvíles

PAMPANEIRA

Pitres

Fuente

Busquístar

Granada

Ferreirola

Mecina-
Fondales

THE HIGH
ALPUJARRAS

Almeria and there were several skirmishes in the hills. In the years that followed this turmoil, the peasants of the Alpujarras suffered severe poverty–even today, most of the subsistence farming is carried out without the aid of machinery–but the recent advent of tourism has brought some money into the area.

The soil is still fertile and crops such as beans, chestnuts and cherries are grown on the terraces. Look out for local produce, including a wide variety of berries, in the markets and grocery shops. Small herds of goats and sheep are moved between village and pasture and, in the evening, traffic jams can occur in the narrow lanes of a village when a pack of laden mules encounters a shepherd's flock. Each village is a maze of such lanes, usually with only one car-carrying road leading in or out. The lanes weave between, through or under whitewashed houses of irregular shapes; you will often pause to wonder whether you're intruding in someone's private courtyard. *Tinaos* or terraces overflowing with geraniums decorate the exterior, along with strings of red peppers hung out to dry in the autumn sun. The Berber influence is visible in the locally woven hangings which cover the doorways during the warmer months. The stone walls of the houses are thick enough to protect from the intense heat of summer and the worst winter storms. The roofs here are flat with tall round chimneys: a style not found elsewhere in Spain but matching the architecture across the straits in the Rif mountains of Morocco. The roof is formed with chestnut beams, over which large slabs of stone are laid. On top is spread a layer of *launa*, flaky grey mica which is traditionally laid during the waning of the moon.

Walking is not especially known as a pastime in Spain and the paths are not well waymarked for the purpose. The suggested route comprises *caminos* –old trading paths–with some forestry tracks and minor roads. It is not a particularly difficult route but a good map is invaluable. It begins with a walk from the whitewashed village of Capileira up the Poqueira ravine (or *barranco*) and back down to another of the *pueblos biancos*, Pampaneira. The second day finds you passing above the top of the Barranco de la Sangre and descending through smaller, less touristed villages to the beautiful lower valley of the Río Trevélez with its pockets of lush vegetation. On the third day, you climb and then contour around the lower slopes of Mulhacén, travelling up the main Trevélez valley to this high mountain settlement, from where a day can be spent walking further up river for dramatic views of the Sierra Nevada mountains. Finally, the route traverses the Barranco de los Castaños and contours the Cerillo Redondo to reach the village of Juvíles.

In the plaza of each village you are sure to find a *fuente* or spring marked either *agua potable* or *no potable* depending on whether or not the water is suitable for drinking. All the villages suggested for overnight stays have shops, often including a *panaderia* (bakery), a *mantequeria* (delicatessen) and *la tienda de comestibles* (grocery). You should buy provisions for lunch each morning as, with the exception of Day 2, there are no shops to be encountered during the day.

Mules are used by locals to transport produce and supplies from one village to another.

DAY ONE - CAPILEIRA TO PAMPANEIRA (10.5 KM; 5 HRS)

Our route begins in Capileira, at 1436 m the highest of the three village in the Poqueira gorge. It clings to the lower slopes of the second highest mountain of the Sierra Nevada, the Veleta. Each year on the 5th of August, a *romerías* or pilgrimage sets forth from Capileira to climb the mountain. Lower down on the same slope lie the similarly pretty villages of Bubión and Pampaneira, the eventual destination for today, following a walk up the valley and back down along the lovely Río Poqueira. Capileira, which is on the Historical Villages list, repays close inspection. It has several noteworthy fuentes and commanding views over the Tajo del Diablo (Devil's Cut) from the lower village. Capileira is today a centre for artists and has a small museum containing articles related to Pedro Alarcón, who wrote about his travels to the Alpujarras in the 19th century.

From the village bus stop, walk along Calle del Dr Castilla, then right along Calle Castillo and take the track that leaves the village from the upper barrio *(quarter) and heads uphill. Ten minutes or so up this cobbled mule path, you pass a water supply hut and the path zigzags right then left up to another water supply hut five minutes on. Turn left and follow the path by the acequia. The path crosses the acequia, becomes a rough vehicle track and then crosses back. A vehicular track comes in from the right and you turn left to join this. This road continues through the hamlet of La Cebadilla to a bridge over the Río Poqueira*

A view of Capileira, the highest village in the Poqueira valley.

which you cross. Upstream a short distance is a hydroelectric power station, where the road ends. From the far side of the bridge, turn left up a steep drive. After ten minutes there is a sharp right-hand bend; take the footpath on the left which passes below a house. Ignore any minor paths off to the left or right and continue down the valley. Approximately 45 minutes from the power station, you pass just above an era or threshing platform and then descend through woodland. Look out for red waymarks, leading you around an old rockfall. Within sight of a bridge, a path up to the right takes you across an era. Turn left down to the bridge, which is a good swimming spot.

After crossing the bridge, walk uphill for five minutes, reaching a Y-junction. The left fork leads back to Capileira. Instead, take the right fork down past a cortijo or farmhouse and into woodland. Turn right by a stream and then sharp left and right again at a T-junction. You should soon reach the lower Capileira bridge: cross this and, after five minutes, turn left on a cobbled uphill section and head down valley. After a couple of minutes, keep left, taking the lower and better used of two paths. Keep to this path, presently passing below an animal shelter, descending steeply and skirting a land slip. After crossing a ditch, ignore a steeply climbing path and instead keep left, descending to the Barranco de Rosas. Soon after crossing the bottom of the gully, turn left along an acequia and after five minutes or so descend left of an era. After zigzagging and crossing another small acequia with black pipes, the path passes between buildings of another ruined cortijo and you keep right, ignoring a narrower path which branches left. In a few minutes, keep right on an upper path. Turn left at a junction immediately before a stream. The path descends, crosses the Bubión bridge and ascends towards Bubión, passing above a ruined watermill.

The village skylines are characterised by tall chimneys and flat roofs.

Bubión is another pretty whitewashed village with a 16th century church and, beside it, remnants of a Nazrid Arab tower. *Once you've explored Bubión, the path which descends to Pampaneira can be found from the Plaza Iglesia (the church square): keep to the left of this late Baroque church and find the Calle Bario Bajo leading off to the left. Pampaneira is reached after 15 minutes or so.*

Like Capileira, Pampaneira is on the Historical Villages list and is worth exploring at leisure. It is well supplied with delightful *fuentes* and, like most villages on this walk, it also has a *lavanderia* or public wash house for laundry. Above the village lies the Buddhist monastery of Al Atalaya, which was founded when the child destined to be the next Dalai Lama in Tibet was born to a Spanish couple in the Poqueira.

DAY TWO - PAMPANEIRA TO BUSQUISTAR VIA PITRES (12 KM; 6 HRS)

Today's route takes you back through Bubión, over a spur to the village of Pitres and then downhill to the delightfully remote hamlets of Mecina Fondales and Ferreirola. The day's destination is Busquistar, an unspoiled village in a fertile setting.

Leave Pampaneira and walk back to Bubión along the footpath taken yesterday. The path to Pitres starts from the main road in Bubión as a cobbled lane opposite the Fuenfria bar. Fork right after a few minutes; the path has white-on-green waymarks. Cross a gravel drive, following the marks and red arrows. In five minutes turn right onto a sealed road (Europe's highest road, over the Sierra Nevada to Granada) and admire the wonderful views. After about 15 minutes on a left hand hairpin bend, turn right onto a gravel drive. Ignoring another gravel road up to the left, continue for about 15 minutes, take a left fork and in a further ten minutes come to a five way meeting of paths. Take the first path to the left. Follow it for 25 to 30 minutes, and turn down right onto a path (the turn-off is just beyond a fence which continues on the right of the drive beyond two buildings). Cross an acequia, turn left downhill, pass a small waterfall and a small sluice and follow the path left away from the acequia and to the hamlet of Capilerilla. After wending a way through the lanes and buildings of Capilerilla, Pitres is ten minutes away, on a well-used path along a shallow gully.

After looking around Pitres, find the walled path passing behind the hotel (Bar la Carretera). It descends sharply, reaching the upper of Mecina-Fondales' three barrios after 20 minutes. Keeping left of a large era, descend between the houses and then right onto a concrete lane. Make your way down to the middle barrio (sometimes called Mecinilla) then continue down via a lane which becomes a steep path to reach a small carpark. From here the lowest of Mecina-Fondales' three barrios–a particularly secluded and picturesque hamlet–may be explored. The next destination is the beautiful hamlet of Ferreirola, thought to be the oldest village in the Alpujarras. Return to where you first reached the car park. Walk under a balcony and wind between houses, then turn left at a T-junction of lanes by an olive grove. Keep left at a fork shortly after bridging a small stream and after walking for about eight minutes beyond the bridge, keep left at a path junction and follow the path up to Ferreirola.

To reach Busquístar via the Rio Trevélez gorge, leave the settlement on the obvious path through orchard groves. After five minutes you reach an effervescent artesian well, tiled with scenes of viticulture. In a further five minutes, views open out of the Trevélez valley, looking back down to Ferreirola, Mecina-Fondales and Pitres. Large rock slabs hereabouts provide an ideal spot for a picnic lunch. Shortly beyond here head down right at a path junction (the upper left path could alternatively be taken directly to Busquístar) and in about ten minutes come to a bridge over the Río Trevélez with a watermill on the near side and a small hydroelectric power station on the far side, both abandoned. After examining these, retrace your steps from the bridge for 30 metres and turn up right on a mule track zigzagging past the front of the mill. In 15 minutes this path meets up with the path coming direct from Ferreirola. Turn right for Busquístar, reached in about 25 minutes.

The name Busquístar derives from the Arabic for 'hidden garden'; it is set in a well-irrigated gully which is shaded by groves of almond trees and poplars. Accommodation in the village is very limited: there is a simple inn above the main bar, with cooking facilities but no restaurant. If necessary, you could continue on the road 2 km to the village of Portugos for the night (see Day 3).

DAY THREE - BUSQUISTAR TO TREVELEZ (13.5 KM; 4.5 HRS)

This day's journey leads you along a sealed but quiet road to the bustling

Some old cortijos are still used as temporary accommodation; others now lie abandoned.

village of Portugos and then up and around the lower slopes of Mulhacén on an unsealed track. The perched mountain village of Trevélez is approached through terraced land farmed using traditional methods. There is nowhere to buy food after Portugos.

The 2 km of road between Busquístar and Portugos passes through expansive chestnut tree woods with views back over the grey launa roofs of Busquístar. After about 20 minutes, detour down the flight of steps to the Fuente Agria ('bitter spring') to which Spanish tourists come to fill their bottles. Nearby, a larger flight of steps lead down to El Chorreón, a delightful stream with iron-stained waterfalls. Portugos is a few minutes further along the road.

In the Plaza Nueva in front of the Hostal Mirador is sign which indicates the road to Trevélez which leaves Portugos in an east northeast direction. On the first part of the route there are many short cuts cutting out some of the hairpin bends as the road ascends. They become increasingly overgrown as height is gained and are not described here but are shown on the map. After the first bend following the 1600 m contour, there is a prominent road junction; turn right (left leads to Capileira). At about the 1700 m contour, it is worthwhile detouring on a track up to the left to the Cortijo de la Sacrista. Sited below wooded rock outcrops and with beautiful views out to the Río Trevélez valley, this would make a pleasant picnic spot. Returning to the road, proceed for a further 15 minutes or so and take a sharp left turn off the road. After five minutes you pass

Traditional farming methods are still used in the Alpujarras.

The highest point of the walk is a remote cortijo on the slopes of the Alcazabar, high up near the source of the Rio Trevélez.

a fenced, cultivated area, beyond which is a clump of trees where a right fork is taken. After a few minutes of level walking you come to a stand of poplars fringing a shaded pond with water flowing into it. With similarly fine views and a water supply, this makes a good alternative spot for lunch.

The road can be regained in a few minutes by walking down the hill. Follow the road to Morron de la Vieja, where there is a pine plantation and two sharp bends in the road. Another 20 minutes along the road, you reach a T-junction. To the right, the road leads to Trevélez. Instead, go straight ahead on a narrow but well-defined path which descends towards Trevélez and meets the road again *later. Across the road, pick up the path again. It ascends and then levels off, contouring around the valley of the Río Chico before descending to the uppermost of Trevélez' three barrios, a feature which gives the village its name.*

Trevélez is claimed to be the highest village in Spain, perched on the flank of Mulhacén which is, at 3479 m, the highest peak on the Iberian peninsula. A romerías in honour of the Virgin of the Snows leaves Trevélez for Mulhacén at midnight on August 5th each year. The village is justly renowned for its cured ham, *jamón serrano*, which is dried in the cold mountain air, and for its excellent markets, held each Wednesday.

DAY FOUR - CAMINO DE LA SIERRA: DAY RETURN (15.5 KM; 5.5 HRS)

The Camino de la Sierra is one of the Sierra Nevada's most ancient (and, in past times, important) trade routes as it could be negotiated by pack animals. It links the Alpujarras with Guadix to the north and is still used to explore the highest peaks of the range. On most days, however, the only people you will encounter are lone herders heading back from Trevélez to their isolated cortijos. The first section of the camino, described here as a return day-walk, is a very scenic valley path leading up the Río Trevélez to the confluence of two of its tributaries, the Río Jumillas and the Río del Puerto de Jeres. At this turning point, a height of 2000 m is reached.

The path leads from the eastern part of Trevélez' middle barrio, passing above the sports ground. After about ten minutes and shortly before the Río Trevélez, take the left fork, remaining on the west bank. Ignore two bridges and continue walking for an hour or so, when you should meet the main acequia taking water to Trevélez. Cross the bridge over the river and continue upstream on the east bank, past the confluence of the Río Culo Perro and into the 1400-sq-km Parque Natural Sierra Nevada. Ignore two more bridges and continue along the east bank through a wire gate. About 25 minutes on, the valley opens out into lush meadowland before closing in once more. Cross to the west bank and, ten minutes later, cross back again. Half an hour on, you reach the confluence of the two main tributaries of the Río Trevélez, near which are several buildings. There are some shady riverside spots here which are ideal for a picnic.

The path crosses the right hand tributary, Río del Puerto de Jeres, and then climbs the hill. Take this path for 15 minutes and then pause for a view of the northeast face of the Alcazabar which suitably translates as 'fortress'. Return to Trevélez by the same route, allowing 2.5 hours for the return journey.

DAY FIVE - TREVELEZ TO JUVILES (9.5 KM; 3.5 HRS)

The final day's route crosses a gully, the Barranco de los Castaños, and contours a spur of Peña de los Papos, from where there are views south to another mountain range before you descend to the pretty village of Juvíles.

Leave Trevélez by Carretera de Ugijar (GR421), the road leading to Juvíles. Just past the walled cemetery, a broad path leads off to the left. This path ascends for approximately 1.5 hours through forest to reach a firebreak. During this time, ignore any left forks, one of which leads to Bérchules. The path follows the fire-

A lone cowherd makes the journey between village and high pasture.

155

break through pine forest and around a hill at about 1700 m. The path then tends gradually easterly and, after 30 minutes or so, ends at a vehicular track which you cross to a narrow path. Hereabouts is the high point of the route (around 1750 m) which provides panoramic views of the walls of Sierra del la Contraviesa, a lesser range to the south. *From here, the descent to Juvíles takes approximately an hour and is quite straightforward.*

Juvíles is an attractive narrow village stretched along the road. Its church, surrounded by gardens, remains in its original un-whitewashed state as do many of the houses nearby. These buildings give an impression of how the villages of the Alpujarras would have appeared some fifty years ago before whitewashing became popular. The village was a centre of silk production during the Moorish period and was the site of atrocities committed by the Christian army against the Moriscos, but now has a more relaxed air.

Notes on the High Alpujarras

TYPE OF WALK	One way, with a day-walk included
LENGTH OF WALK	61 kilometres (38 miles); five days
DIFFICULTY	An easy-to-medium grade walk, with some steep terrain
START	Capileira, in the Poqueira Valley
FINISH	Juvíles, a western village in the High Alpujarras

PUBLIC TRANSPORT
By bus from the Alsina Graells depot in Granada; the journey to Capileira takes 2-3 hours.
A bus from Juvíles returns to Granada, stopping at Trevélez, Bubión and Capileira en route.

LUGGAGE   Leave excess luggage in Granada.

CLIMATE
Between mid-June and late August, the heat can be too taxing for walking. Snow covers the higher hills in winter. The best times for walking are spring and autumn. Take care to use a sunscreen as ultraviolet rays are strong at this altitude.

MAP   Instituto Geografico Nacional / Federacion Espanola de Montanismo *Sierra Nevada* 1:50,000

PATH   A combination of *camino* (old mule routes for trading), forestry roads and minor roads. Carry a compass as paths are not well-marked.

SHORTER VARIANT   (see Days 1 & 2)
A two-day version: *Bus from Granada to Capileira;* 1 - walk from Capileira via Bubión to Pampaneira; 2 - walk from Pampaneira via Pitres to either Busquístar or Portugos; *bus to Granada.*

VILLAGES
Capileira (population 600), Bubión (350), **Pampaneira** (900), Pitres (800), Mecina-Fondales (150), Ferreirola (200), **Busquístar** (700), Portugos (500), **Trevélez** (1150), **Juvíles** (500).

ACCOMMODATION
Inexpensive hostales and pensiones at most of the villages; some hotels at suggested overnight stops. Limited accommodation at Busquistar; none at Mecina-Fondales and Ferreirola. Contact details for some hotels are listed on the back of the *Sierra Nevada* map.

CUISINE
The local delicacy is the cured ham, *jamón serrano*, which is included in many dishes such as *habas con jamón* (with broad beans), *trucha con jamón* (with river trout) and *plato alpujarreño* (a fried platter with black pudding and egg). Also popular are sweet cakes with an Arab influence. *Costa* is the locally produced rosé wine.

WILDLIFE
Many types of butterfly; various birds, including golden eagles, partidges, bee-eaters and hoopoe; Spanish ibex, chamois and wild boar. Beautiful wildflowers in spring, including many gentians. Woods of chestnut, walnut and poplar trees.

SPECIAL FEATURES
The *pueblos biancos* (white villages) of Andalusia; the Poqueira and Trevélez valleys; Moorish *acequias*; the Fuente Agria, a ferruginous spring near Portugos; views of the Sierra Nevada mountains.

FURTHER READING

WALKING IN THE SIERRA NEVADA OF SPAIN
by Andy Walmsley, published by Cicerone Press, 1996.

WALKING IN SPAIN
2nd edition, edited by Miles Robbis, published by Lonely Planet, 1999.

ANDALUCIA
edited by John Noble and Susan Forsyth, published by Lonely Planet, 1999.

USEFUL ADDRESSES

PARQUE NATURAL SIERRA NEVADA CENTRO DE INFORMACION
Plaza de la Libertad, Pampaneira; Tel: 958) 763127

PATRONATO DE TURISMO - the regional tourist office
Plaza Mariana Pineda 10, 18009 Granada; Tel: 958) 223527

LIBRERIA DAURO - a shop which sells maps and local guidebooks
Calle Zacatin 3, Granada

GLOSSARY

acequia   an aqueduct (Spain)

allt   a stream (Scotland)

alp   high summer pasture (German)

alpenglow   light on mountains at sunrise and sunset

auberge   a simple inn (France)

Aussicht   a view (German)

B&B   a home offering bed and breakfast (Britain)

Bach   a stream (German)

Bahnhof   railway station (German)

balcony   a natural terrace high above a valley

barranco   a ravine (Spain)

barrio   a village quarter (Spain)

bastide   a 13th century planned town (France)

beck   a mountain stream (Northern England)

belvedere   a scenic point (Italian, but widely used)

ben   a mountain (Scotland)

Bergweg   a mountain path (German)

bothy   a hut (Scotland)

brae   upper slope (Scotland)

bridleway   a path for walkers, cyclists and horse riders

burn   a mountain stream (Scotland)

buron   a herder's hut found on the French Aubrac

cairn   a heap of stones marking a path or summit

camino   an old trading route (Spain)

canton   a self-governing region (Switzerland)

cascata   a waterfall (Italy)

causse   a limestone plateau

chamois   goat-like antelope (*gemse* in German)

cirque   a rounded, high precipice formed glacially

col   a mountain pass (*collado* in Spain)

contour   to travel across a slope on one level

crête   a ridge (France)

département   an administrative region (France)

dolomite   a hard limestone rock

draille   a drove road (France)

era   a paved threshing platform (Spain)

eremo   a hermitage (Italy)

fells   uplands (Northern England)

fiume   a river (Italy)

forcella   a mountain pass (Italy)

fosse   a canal (Italy)

fuente   a fountain or spring (Spain)

funivia   a cable car (Italy)

Füssweg   a footpath (German)

Gasthaus/Gasthof   a hotel or inn (German)

ghyll or *gill*   a stream or ravine (Northern England)

gîte d'etape   self-catering hostels (France)

glen   a narrow valley (Scotland)

Gletscher   a glacier (German)

grande randonnée (GR)   a long-distance footpath (France)

grüetzi!   greetings! (Swiss German)

grüss Gott!   greetings! (Austrian German)

haus or *hows*   a mountain pass (Northern England)

Höhenweg   a high-level path (German)

Hütte   a mountain hut (German)

karst   limestone affected by underground drainage

Kogel   a hill (German)

lago   a lake (Italy)

linn   a waterfall (Scotland)

loch   a lake (Scotland)

malga   a farm (Italy)

marmot   a large furry rodent found in alpine regions

massif   a high mountain range

moor   high ground ususally covered in heather

Oberland   uplands (German)

ola!   greetings! (Spain)

pass   low ground offering a route between mountains

pian   a high-level plateau (Italy)

pike   pointed mountains (Northern England)

pont / ponte   a bridge (France / Italy)

postbus   a passenger-carrying bus that runs mail routes

potable   suitable for drinking

préalpes   foothills north and south of the Alps

punta   a point of land (Italy)

raptor   a bird of prey

rifugio   a mountain hut (Italy)

rio   a stream or river (Italy and Spain)

rocca   a ruined castle (Italy)

ruisseau   a stream (France)

saddle   a broad dip between two elevations

Scheidegg   a watershed (German)

Schlucht   a gorge (German)

Schloss   a castle (German)

scree   loose rock on a steep slope

See   a lake (German)

sentiero   a footpath (Italy)

sorgente   spring or source of a river (Italy)

spot height   heights marked on a map

strath   a wide river valley (Scotland)

Tal   a valley (German)

tarn   a small mountain lake (Northern Britain)

torrente   a mountain stream (Italy)

transhumance   the seasonal movement of livestock

treeline   the highest level at which forest grows

trig points   surveying posts often marked on maps

tympanum   decorated space above a doorway

via ferrata   a steep route with fixed cables (Italy)

Wald   a forest (German)

Wasser / Wasserfall   water / waterfall (German)

watershed   the ridge dividing two drainage areas

waymark   a symbol indicating a path

Weg   a footpath (German)

Zimmer Frei   rooms available (German)

FURTHER READING

FRANCE ON FOOT
by Bruce Le Favour, published by Attis Press, 1999

A GUIDE TO THE VEGETATION OF BRITAIN & EUROPE
by Oleg Polunin & Martin Walters, published by Oxford University Press, 1985

THE INDEPENDENT WALKER'S GUIDE TO FRANCE / GREAT BRITAIN / ITALY
three books by Frank W. Booth, published by Interlink

THE LONG DISTANCE WALKER'S HANDBOOK
(on Britain) by Carolyn B. Mitchell, published by A&C Black, 1998

A WALKER'S GUIDE TO EUROPE
by A. Howcroft & R. Sale, published by Wildwood House, 1983

WALKING EASY IN THE SWISS & AUSTRIAN ALPS 2/e
by Chet & Carolee Lipton, published by GlobePequot, 1999

WALKING IN BRITAIN / FRANCE / ITALY / SPAIN / SWITZERLAND
a range of titles published by Lonely Planet, Australia

WALKING IN FRANCE
by Rob Hunter, published by Oxford Illustrated Press, UK, 1982

USEFUL ADDRESSES

HOLIDAY OPERATORS - offering luggage-free independent walks in many areas in this book.

Sherpa Expeditions, 131a Heston Rd, Hounslow, Middlesex TW5 ORD, England
internet site: www.sherpa-walking-holidays.co.uk   Tel: 020) 85772717 Fax: 020) 85729788

Ramblers Holidays, Box 43, Welwyn Garden, Hertfordshire AL8 6PQ, England
internet site: www.ramblersholidays.co.uk   Tel: 01707) 331133 Fax: 01707) 333276

Headwater Holidays, 146 London Rd, Northwich, Cheshire CW9 5HH, England
internet site: www.headwater.com   Tel: 01606) 813333 Fax: 01606) 813334

MAP SUPPLIERS - retailers offering mail order:

Elstead Maps, PO Box 52 ELSTEAD, Godalming Surrey GU8 6JJ, England
Tel: 01252) 703472 Fax: 01252) 703971   internet: www.elstead.co.uk

Stanfords Bookshop, 12-14 Long Acre, Covent Garden, London WC2E 9LP Tel: 0171) 8361321

WALKING IN EUROPE - an internet site containing lots of useful information, including contact details for European walking associations. Created by Peter Robins, of the Long Distance Walkers Association.
www.biblioset.demon.co.uk/LDWA/Europe.htm or   www.gorp.com/gorp/activity/europe/Europe.htm

SUMMARY OF WALKS

	DURATION	LEVEL	DESCRIPTION
AUSTRIA			
Salzkammergut	4 walks	easy to moderate	A series of day walks from picturesque Hallstatt deep in Austria's alpine lakes district, featuring exquisite scenery and a rich variety of geological and historical diversions.
FRANCE			
Dordogne	5 days	easy-moderate	A magnificent walk along the paths of the Dordogne river valley, replete with grand castles and fortified bastide towns, ending at the spectacular site of Rocamadour.
Way of St Jacques	6 days	moderate	A pilgrimage route through the Massif Central, crossing the remote Aubrac plateau then descending to the river Lot and the medieval village of Conques.
Verdon Gorge	5 days	difficult	A demanding but unforgettable excursion combining the rugged scenery of Haute Provence's limestone mountains with a descent through Europe's deepest gorge.
GERMANY			
High Black Forest	5 days	easy	A leisurely walk through the charming southern Black Forest along romantic forest paths to glacial lakes, summits and fertile valleys dotted with traditional farmhouses.
Saxon Switzerland	5 days	moderate	A venture into this dramatic region to explore the strange sandstone formations which line the delightful river Elbe.
GREAT BRITAIN			
Heart of Scotland	6 days	moderate	A hike over heather-clad hills and through glens, past deep lochs and into remote countryside of Perthshire.
Lake District	5 days	moderate-difficult	An exhilarating circuit around the heart of Cumbria, encompassing rugged fells, sparkling tarns and quaint villages.
ITALY			
Umbrian Hilltowns	4 days	easy-moderate	A classic walk, rich in history, between two famous hilltowns–Assisi and Spoleto–through the Vale of Spoleto and several of Umbria's less visited hilltown treasures.
Dolomites	5 walks	easy to hard	Awe-inspiring day treks into the north-eastern Dolomites which surround the spectacular town of Cortina d'Ampezzo.
Cinque Terre	4 days	easy	A spectacular coastal and ridge walk linking the impossibly picturesque fishing villages of the Cinque Terre.
SPAIN			
High Alpujarras	5 days	easy-moderate	A walk showcasing the exotic white villages which perch on the southern foothills of the high Sierra Nevada.
SWITZERLAND			
Bernese Alps	5 walks	moderate to hard	Exhilarating day walks from the charming town of Lauterbrunnen, nestling in its perfect glacial valley, around the slopes of Switzerland's most dramatic mountains.